Editor
Walter Kelly, M.A.

Managing Editor
Ina Massler Levin, M.A.

Editor-in-Chief
Sharon Coan, M.S. Ed.

Illustrator
Ken Tunell

Cover Artist
Denise Bauer

Art Coordinator
Kevin Barnes

Art Director
CJae Froshay

Imaging
Rosa C. See

Product Manager
Phil Garcia

Portions used under license from *The World Almanac*. Copyright (c) 2003 World Almanac Education Group, Inc. All Rights Reserved.

Publishers
Rachelle Cracchiolo, M.S. Ed.
Mary Dupuy Smith, M.S. Ed.

Take Five Minutes
Fascinating Facts

Grades 6-8

Authors

Greg Camden, M.A.
Eric Migliaccio

Teacher Created Materials, Inc.

6421 Industry Way
Westminster, CA 92683
www.teachercreated.com

ISBN-0-7439-3793-7

©2003 Teacher Created Materials, Inc.
Made in U.S.A.

Table of Contents

Introduction

The World Almanac spans the curricula—from language arts to science, from social studies to math—and is presented in an information-rich format that encourages analysis and discussion of a multitude of topics. *Take Five Minutes: Fascinating Facts from "The World Almanac"* pulls from this wealth of information and condenses it into five-minute lessons that are stimulating, self-contained, and simple to teach.

What exactly is the Dow Jones? Who holds the title of "the world's fastest human?" How do mountains come to be? What does the number of calories in food actually tell you? Why are Gandhi and Einstein household names? These are the kinds of things that many people remain unsure of right through adulthood, but *Take Five Minutes: Fascinating Facts from "The World Almanac"* answers these questions—and a lot more. From these short lessons, students will be able to gain a basic understanding of many of the processes of our world—from the physical (gravity, the elements) to the societal (voting, taxes); they will learn about things of global consequence (Afghanistan beyond its role in the 9/11 tragedy, why frontier forests are important) alongside things of limited consequence (how best to compare pitchers, where are the world's tallest buildings)—and in all of these they will accrue practice using the essential thinking skills that will help them not only in their future academic careers, but in life as well. Along the way, they will have a chance to pick up some knowledge that they might not have otherwise encountered.

How to Use This Book

The first five minutes of a class are among the most critical in teaching for the role they play in setting the instructional stage and transitioning students into the lesson. *Take Five Minutes: Fascinating Facts from "The World Almanac"* is designed to assist teachers in this task through a variety of engaging activities.

This book is divided into eight sections based on the major content areas presented in *The World Almanac*. Each section begins with a title page that offers a brief look at what is contained on the pages to follow. These sections can be taught as a whole to reinforce a unit of study; or, because the lessons are self-contained, you may teach them in any order. You may even allow the students to pick *The World Almanac* lesson of the day. You might do this by reading out five lesson titles, simply picking them out randomly. Have the students vote on the title that interests them most. Democracy in action!

Although all of the lessons in *Take Five Minutes: Fascinating Facts from "The World Almanac"* are self-contained, an additional feature of this book is that an earlier lesson often provides information that will offer students a fuller understanding of a later lesson. For example, in a Section I lesson on the Nobel Prizes, Albert Einstein is one of the listed winners; Section II contains a lesson about him; and a Section III lesson is on gravity—the understanding of which is one of Einstein's major scientific contributions. This kind of building of a knowledge base is also present within sections. Section I, "World History and Culture," is ordered so that a lesson on the Magna Carta precedes one on the founding of the presidency of the United States—which itself precedes a lesson on the Supreme Court. This ordering is also conceptual: students will have something additional to think about the lesson on award-winning children's books when seeing later in Section V that Lois Lowry's Newbery Medal-winning *The Giver* was one of the 50 books most subject to banning efforts in the 1990s. However, as stated above, these lessons are not interdependent—and so the choice is yours!

Introduction *(cont.)*

How to Use this Book *(cont.)*

Each of the lessons in *Take Five Minutes: Fascinating Facts from "The World Almanac"* employs a combination of four different components:

1. **Reading Passages**—Every lesson in this book involves students in using skills and strategies of the reading process to interpret and understand text. The topics explored in *Take Five Minutes: Fascinating Facts from "The World Almanac"* range from the infinite (the universe) to the infinitesimal (atoms)—and cover much in between.

2. **Charts and Graphs**—The majority of the lessons in this book contain a chart or graph of some kind, whether it be a chart, bar graph, table, or time line. Because charts and graphs are invaluable when comparing data, textbooks and reference books such as almanacs are replete with them—and so students need to be comfortable with reading and processing these effective and efficient organizational tools.

3. **Encapsulated Facts**—Many of the lessons contain sidebars—paragraphs entitled "It's a Fact!"—that offer interesting information that supplements the main text on the page. These sidebars teach students to process information from different textual formats—and they do so in a self-contained manner that augments the learning of the lesson without seeming to do so by capitalizing on the manner of picking up trivia that tends to stick with middle-schoolers.

4. **Comprehension and Critical-Thinking Questions**—Each lesson ends with a section entitled "Questions to Ponder." This section contains five questions that get progressively more difficult. For instance, the first question usually involves simple recall of a fact presented in the text, whereas the fourth question will ask them to process and apply the information they just read. The fifth and final question generally asks the student to relate the information in the lesson to events in his or her life and the way in which they view the world in light of the topic at hand. In this way, critical-thinking skills are developed and/or honed. Overall, the questions are varied so as to avoid repetition and to promote learning. There are math questions included in history lessons and language arts incorporated into science sections. All of this helps to keep your students focused, motivated, and learning. (See pages 93–96 for a complete answer key.)

Additional Activities

The lessons in this book offer several opportunities for you to allow your students to apply the knowledge they will gain, while at the same time reinforcing a particular writing or math concept from your daily lessons.

- Have each student write one complete sentence about the subject just discussed. Specify whether the sentence needs to contain an adverb, a prepositional phrase, an appositive, etc.

- Have each student create a complete sentence that uses a particular vocabulary word from the lesson just discussed.

- Have each student create a math problem, the answer to which is an important statistic from the lesson just discussed.

- As an extra-credit opportunity, allow students to write a lesson that might fit into *Take Five Minutes: Fascinating Facts from "The World Almanac."* Make sure the lesson includes text, a chart illustrating the text, and questions that test comprehension of the lesson and also expand the reader's thoughts about the subject being discussed.

Meeting Standards

Each lesson in *Take Five Minutes: Fascinating Facts from "The World Almanac"* meets one or more of the following standards, which are used with permission from McREL (copyright 2000 McREL, Mid-continent Research for Education and Learning. Telephone: 303-337-0990. Web site: *www.mcrel.org*).

The Arts

- Understands the context in which theatre, film, television, and electronic media are performed today as well as in the past

Mathematics

- Uses a variety of strategies in the problem-solving process
- Understands and applies basic and advanced properties of the concepts of numbers
- Uses basic and advanced procedures while performing the processes of computation
- Understands and applies basic and advanced properties of the concepts of geometry
- Understands and applies basic and advanced concepts of statistics and data analysis
- Understands and applies basic and advanced concepts of measurement

Science

- Understands atmospheric processes and the water cycle
- Understands Earth's composition and structure
- Understands the composition and structure of the universe and Earth's place in it
- Understands the relationships among organisms and their physical environment
- Understands the structure and properties of matter
- Understands the sources and properties of energy
- Understands forces and motion
- Understands the nature of scientific knowledge
- Understands the nature of scientific inquiry

History

- Understands and knows how to analyze chronological relationships and patterns
- Understands the institutions and practice of government created during the revolution and how these elements were revised between 1787 and 1815 to create the foundation of the American political system based on the U.S. Constitution and the Bill of Rights
- Understands how the Cold War and conflicts in Korea and Vietnam influenced domestic and international politics
- Understands developments in foreign and domestic policies between the Nixon and Clinton presidencies
- Understands economic, social, and cultural developments in the contemporary United States
- Understands major global trends since World War II

Meeting Standards *(cont.)*

Language Arts

- Uses reading skills and strategies to understand and interpret a variety of informational texts

Civics

- Understands ideas about civic life, politics, and government
- Understands the sources, purposes, and functions of law and the importance of the rule of law for the protection of individual rights and the common good
- Understands alternative forms of representation and how they serve the purposes of constitutional government
- Understands the central ideas of American constitutional government and how this form of government has shaped the character of American society

Technology

- Knows the characteristics and uses of computer hardware and operating systems
- Understands the relationships among science, technology, society, and the individual
- Understands the nature of technological design
- Understands the nature and uses of different forms of technology

Life Skills

- Understands and applies basic principles of logic and reasoning
- Effectively uses mental processes that are based on identifying similarities and differences (compares, contrasts, classifies)
- Applies decision-making techniques

Economics

- Understands basic features of market structures and exchanges
- Understands basic concepts about international economics

Geography

- Knows the location of places, geographic features, and patterns of the environment
- Understands the physical and human characteristics of places
- Understands the concepts of regions
- Knows the physical processes that shape patterns on Earth's surface
- Understands the characteristics of ecosystems on Earth's surface
- Understands the nature and complexity of Earth's cultural mosaics
- Understands the forces of cooperation and conflict that shape the divisions of Earth's surface
- Understands how human actions modify the physical environment
- Understands how physical systems affect human systems
- Understands global development and environmental issues

Health

- Understands essential concepts about nutrition and health

World History and Culture

Talk Is Old

Over 6,000 languages are spoken in the world today, but it wasn't always so. Although no one is sure exactly how language began, it is known that languages have evolved over time, and that, if you go back far enough, many of them have common roots.

The languages of the world are grouped into *language families*. The languages in a particular family are just like people in a family: they are different, but they come from common ancestors. So, each language family can be traced back to *ancestor languages*. Since language existed long before there were written documents, scholars cannot be sure exactly how languages developed before a certain point. Because of this, these ancestor languages have been lost. Even so, linguists (people who study languages) can study how languages have evolved over thousands of years. By studying how languages of today have changed over time, linguists can see which ones came from common ancestors. They have found that language seems to have developed in several different areas of the world that were cut off from each other. This is why it seems that not all languages share a single common ancestor language. Since language developed before people could travel far or communicate with others who lived far away, the farther apart two areas were, the greater the difference in languages. Over thousands of years, people who lived in one area would spread out, and over time the ancestor language they had once shared became many different languages. However, since these languages shared a common root, they would be similar in some ways. This is how language families came to be. Today there are over 100 language families.

Major Languages in the World Today

Language	# Speakers*	Language Family	Language	# Speakers*	Language Family
Mandarin**	874 million	Sino-Tibetan	Japanese	125 million	Altaic
Hindi	366 million	Indo-European	German	100 million	Indo-European
English	341 million	Indo-European	Korean	78 million	Altaic
Spanish	335 million	Indo-European	French	77 million	Indo-European
Arabic	207 million	Semitic	Wu**	77 million	Sino-Tibetan
Bengali	207 million	Indo-European	Javanese	75 million	Malayo-Polynesian
Portuguese	176 million	Indo-European	Yue**	71 million	Sino-Tibetan
Russian	167 million	Indo-European	Telugu	69 million	Dravidian

*speakers whose first language this is
**different forms of Chinese

Questions to Ponder

1. What is a language family?

2. How many ancestor languages are spoken today?

3. If each language family had the same number of languages in it, about how many languages would be in each family?

4. There are many different forms of Chinese. More than _____ people speak Chinese in the world today. (*Fill in the blank.*)

5. What foreign language would you most like to learn to speak? Why? Do you think it would be very much like English? Why or why not?

The First Bill of Rights

On June 15, 1215, England's King John approved the Magna Carta, a document that granted to his subjects a great many rights and that put the law of the land above any one person—including the king himself! This document is still considered to be one of the most important in the history of human rights.

In the years just prior to the Magna Carta, to support a failing war with France, King John had been demanding more and more taxes without the barons' consent, which was a violation of English custom. Because of this, the barons (at the time, 25 men providing the king with military and other services in exchange for land and protection) threatened to rebel. To satisfy them, he agreed to the Magna Carta, a document comprised of 63 "liberties." These included freedom of the church, equal access for all to the court system, certain rights regarding imprisonment, and a fair system of taxes. Perhaps most important in the document, though, was a part that held the king himself subject to the rules set out in the Magna Carta—the first time in history that such a thing had been done. The idea that no one—not even the king—is above the law, along with the idea that all citizens are "granted, for us and our heirs for ever, all the liberties written out below, to have and to keep for them and their heirs, of us and our heirs," became the foundation for future English law. The effect of the Magna Carta was so profound that, over 500 years later, the U.S. Constitution and Bill of Rights were modeled on it. When the Universal Declaration of Human Rights was written in 1948, it was called "a Magna Carta for all humanity."

> ✧✧✧**It's a Fact!**✧✧✧
>
> *Magna Carta* is Latin for "great charter (contract)." The document was written in Latin, the language in which most English official documents— especially legal and religious ones— were written. This practice survives today to a certain degree, in that many Latin terms are permanent parts of legal terminology used in both England and the U.S.

Questions to Ponder

1. What is another common word for "liberties"?

2. About how many centuries have passed since the signing of the Magna Carta? (Round to the nearest whole century.)

3. What does "terminology" mean? What part of this word gives you a clue to its meaning?

4. From this article, can you tell how long England has existed? If you can, *how* can you tell; and if you can't, is there *anything* you can tell about how long England has existed?

5. Do you think the Magna Carta was an important document? Why or why not?

Afghanistan: Surviving Oppression

THE WORLD ALMANAC

In September of 2001, Afghanistan rose to prominence in the collective mind of the world due to the fact that the Taliban, Afghanistan's ruling power at the time, harbored al-Qaeda, the terrorist organization responsible for the 9/11 attacks. Many people in the U.S. blamed the entire country of Afghanistan, not understanding that the Taliban were an oppressive government and represented only a small fraction of the country's people. Unfortunately, the Taliban were only the most-recent example of a long history of oppression suffered by Afghanistan's people.

From the earliest of times, foreign powers have continually invaded Afghanistan, wanting to rule the country mostly because of the Khyber Pass, a natural route running through the towering Hindu Kush mountain range that has been used for trade and military strategy. In more recent times, Britain and then Russia invaded Afghanistan.

In 1919 Afghanistan finally won independence from Britain, and its people enjoyed a progressive leadership through 1973, when a military coup overthrew the monarchy. By 1978, the Soviet Union had taken over Afghanistan and did not leave for over a decade. When they finally withdrew, there was a bloody civil war, from which the Taliban, an ultra-conservative Islamic group, emerged victorious. The Taliban immediately instituted oppressive policies, which included destroying all non-Islamic religious artifacts (Afghanistan's religious history consists of Islam, Buddhism, and Zoroastrianism), banning television, and stripping from women basically all rights.

◇◇◇**It's a Fact!**◇◇◇

An *afghan* is a knitted and sewn woolen blanket or shawl. This word came to be because Afghan needlework has been well-respected for centuries.

After 9/11, a U.S.-led coalition—including many Afghans who had struggled for decades to bring democracy and justice to their country—overthrew the Taliban, allowing a government representative of the Afghan people to come into power. Although Afghanistan has been sorely stressed by centuries of warfare, its culture reflects its ancient roots. Afghanistan contains striking architectural remnants of all ages, including Greek and Buddhist shrines, and monasteries, arches, monuments, and mosques. One of Afghanistan's most famous statues, the Great Buddha of Bamian, was carved in stone and stood 55 meters high. Unfortunately, it was destroyed by the Taliban and their supporters.

Little that Afghans make is unattractive, as embroidery, calligraphy, graphic arts, and poetry are revered in Afghanistan, and other fine work in illustration, bronze, stone, tile, and wood has continued to flourish. Gold and silver jewelry, marvelous decorative embroidery, and various leather goods are still made in homes. But by far the most famous art the country produces is its Afghan rugs, known and desired the world over.

Questions to Ponder

1. For how many years in the 20th century was Afghanistan independent of being ruled by other countries?
2. What does "prominence" mean?
3. What is a coalition?
4. Name two geographic features of Afghanistan.
5. Do you think it is justified for one country to invade another? Explain.

The Birth of the Presidency

THE WORLD ALMANAC

George Washington was not a man who sought power. However, once the United States had gained independence from England, it was felt that he was the only one who was widely-respected enough to be the new country's first president, and so he reluctantly took the job once he had been voted into office.

Washington was very careful and thoughtful about everything he did while president, understanding that his actions would shape the presidency for all future generations. "I walk on untrodden ground [ground that has not been walked upon before]," he said. "There is scarcely any part of my conduct which may not hereafter be drawn in precedent [be used as a guide for the future]." With this in mind, Washington made sure not to use his power and popularity to force Congress, which was very weak in its early years, to go along with him. He did this because he believed very strongly in the independence of the three branches of government as outlined in the Constitution.

Washington agreed to serve a second term only because it was believed that the nation was not yet strong enough to survive a change of leadership. After his second term, however, he would not take on a third, fearing that to do so would make the presidency resemble a monarchy—the very thing the Founding Fathers wished to avoid. His last act as president was yet one more precedent: to let the Constitutional transfer of power take place. After Washington's death, John Adams, the man who had followed him as president, spoke of the great model Washington had been: "His example is now complete, and it will teach wisdom and virtue to magistrates, citizens, and men, not only in the present age but in future generations as long as our history shall be read."

◆◆◆It's a Fact!◆◆◆

Only one president, Franklin D. Roosevelt, has served more than two terms: he died in office in 1944, not long after being elected to his fourth. Although by this time there was no danger of presidents becoming like kings, since then an amendment to the Constitution allows the president to serve only a maximum of two terms.

Questions to Ponder

1. Why was Washington so careful and thoughtful about what he did while he was president?

2. Why was Washington sure not to use his power to force Congress to do what he wanted?

3. If people say they are reluctant to do something, what do they mean?

4. In his era, what is the longest time Washington could have served as president by law?

5. How do you think the country might have been different if Washington had been more interested in power than he was?

The Law of the Land

The United States government has three branches: the executive, the legislative, and the judicial. The last one of these is comprised of the court system, and the head of this is the Supreme Court. The Supreme Court was established by the Constitution. Its purpose is to be the final say in most legal matters, including how to interpret the Constitution and to decide disputes between other branches of government. Once the Supreme Court makes a decision, that decision is final, and only a Constitutional amendment or a later ruling by the Court itself can change a Supreme Court decision.

The Court is made up of one chief justice and eight associate justices. They are nominated by the president but must be approved by the Senate. Once appointed to serve on the Court, they remain for life (or until they choose to retire). The idea is that justices are supposed to be beyond being influenced by any outside forces when deciding cases. A justice does not have to answer to anyone except his or her fellow justices.

The Court's term begins the first Monday in October and usually runs through June. Many cases are brought to the Court—all of them having wound their way through lower courts—but the Court will agree to hear only some of the cases, sending the rest back because the Court feels they do not meet the specific criteria for being considered.

After hearing a case, the justices debate among themselves and vote. Then, the justices publish their decision in writing. If a vote is unanimous (9–0), only one opinion (a legal explanation of the decision) is written. However, if the vote is split, often two opinions, the majority and minority, are written—but the majority opinion is the law.

Some Major Supreme Court Decisions

Name of Case (Year)	Result of Decision
Marbury v. Madison (1803)	Court could rule acts of Congress unconstitutional.
McCulloch v. Maryland (1819)	Defined the power of Congress.
Gitlow v. New York (1925)	States could not infringe upon free speech.
Brown v. Board of Education (1954)	Made school segregation illegal.
Mapp v. Ohio (1961)	Evidence obtained from illegal search cannot be used.
Gideon v. Wainwright (1963)	Entitled defendants to an attorney, even if they could not afford one.
Miranda v. Ohio (1966)	All criminal suspects must be read rights before being questioned.
Loving v. Virginia (1967)	Made bans on interracial marriages illegal.
U.S. v. Nixon (1974)	Even the president must provide evidence if needed for a criminal trial.

Questions to Ponder

1. The Supreme Court heads which branch of the U.S. government?

2. About how long is the Court's term each year?

3. Why are the Supreme Court justices appointed for life?

4. When a person is arrested, which Supreme Court decision ensures that person will be told his or her rights before police questioning? Which one ensures the person will get a lawyer at public expense if he or she cannot afford one?

5. Do you think that a court with the final say in all legal and Constitutional matters and whose members are appointed for life is a good idea? Explain your answer.

The Great Soul

Throughout history, revolution usually comes about by force and violence, at the cost of many lives. However, there are other ways. One of the best examples of this is Mohandas K. Gandhi, who came to be called *mahatma* ("great soul") by his Indian countrymen for his efforts on their behalf. Because of his leadership, India gained its freedom—and did so without violence.

As a young man, Gandhi practiced law in South Africa. While there, he was disgusted and angered at the lack of civil rights given to certain racial groups, and so he began to fight against the government and to motivate other people to help him do so. Instead of violence, Gandhi preached non-cooperation and passive resistance. This meant that, while he and his allies would not fight, they also would not obey. The result was that they would often practice civil disobedience—drawing attention to the injustice of certain laws by breaking those laws and willingly accepting imprisonment or other punishment that followed. This became very effective once enough people were willing to participate, because the people far outnumbered the police and government officials. During the 20 years he lived in South Africa, he was able to get the government to make many changes.

Later, Gandhi returned to live in India. At the time, India was ruled by Great Britain, and Gandhi used many of the same practices (which he called *Satyagraha*, a Sanskrit word meaning "truth and firmness") to help get India's freedom. He organized strikes, marches, and protest gatherings to show the British government that it could not control the Indian people. Although the British jailed Gandhi several times, it could not stop his independence movement. Eventually, he succeeded in forcing the British to grant India its independence. The Great Soul had led a successful revolution without ever firing a shot or striking a blow.

> ◇◇◇**It's a Fact!**◇◇◇
>
> In the United States, Martin Luther King, Jr. employed many of Gandhi's practices in the black civil-rights movement of the 1950s and '60s. Gandhi himself was influenced by the teachings of Jesus and Buddha and the writings of Leo Tolstoy and Henry David Thoreau—particularly Thoreau's essay "Civil Disobedience."

Questions to Ponder

1. From which country did Gandhi help India gain its independence?

2. In what foreign country did Gandhi live for a long period? Why did he go there originally?

3. Instead of violence, what did Gandhi use to bring about change?

4. What is "passive resistance"?

5. Gandhi felt violence was never justified in any conflict. During World War II, many people felt Gandhi was wrong about this when it came to fighting countries like Nazi Germany. Do you think Gandhi was right, or do you think there are some situations in which violence is the only way? Explain your answer.

The Nobel Prizes

Most people have heard of "the Nobel Prize," but many do not realize that there are five Nobel Prizes—one each for physics, chemistry, physiology or medicine, literature, and peace. Since 1901, these five Nobel Prizes have been awarded almost every year.

The prizes are named after Swedish chemist and engineer Alfred B. Nobel (1833–1896). Nobel, who spoke five languages and whose interests ranged from the sciences to poetry and philosophy, became fascinated in his late 20s with safely harnessing the power of nitroglycerin, an unpredictable liquid explosive. With the successful invention of dynamite, he became rich, establishing 90 factories and laboratories in over 20 different countries. However, he could not prevent his discovery from being used just for its intended purposes (to safely and inexpensively blast away earth and rock in the construction of roads, tunnels, etc.), but also for violent ones, leading to a French newspaper labeling Nobel the "merchant of death."

◆◆◆It's a Fact!◆◆◆

A sixth prize, the Nobel Memorial Prize in Economic Science, is not officially a Nobel Prize. It was established in 1968 by the Bank of Sweden and is administered by the Royal Swedish Academy of Sciences—the same organization that hands out the Nobel Prizes in Physics and Chemistry.

The truth is that Nobel was a lifelong pacifist. In his will, he bequeathed the equivalent of $9 million (94% of his estate at the time of his death) for the establishment of prizes that now bear his name, instructing that the interest on this sum each year be given to those judged to have most benefited humankind in each of the aforementioned areas.

It was important to Nobel that the prizes be awarded with complete impartiality. "It is my express wish that in awarding the prizes no consideration whatever shall be given to the nationality of the candidates," Nobel wrote in his will, "so that the most worthy shall receive the prize, whether he be a Scandinavian or not."

Selected Nobel Prize Winners

Recipient (Nationality)	Prize	Year	Recipient (Nationality)	Prize	Year
Kofi Annan (Ghana)	Peace	2001	William Faulkner (U.S.)	Literature	1949
Jimmy Carter (U.S.)	Peace	2002	Mikhail S. Gorbachev (U.S.S.R.)	Peace	1990
Marie Curie (France, Poland)	Physics (shared w/ two others)	1903	Martin Luther King, Jr. (U.S.)	Peace	1964
	Chemistry	1911	Ivan P. Pavlov (Russia)	Phys./Med.	1904
Albert Einstein (Germany, U.S.)	Physics	1921	Jean-Paul Sartre (France)	Literature (declined)	1964

Questions to Ponder

1. What is a pacifist?

2. What was Nobel's total estate worth (in U.S. currency) upon his death?

3. What does "bequeath" mean?

4. Which of the prizewinners listed above have dual nationalities?

5. Jean-Paul Sartre declined to accept his Nobel Prize, and he is not the only person to do so. Why do you think he might have done this? Are there any reasons that you would decline a prestigious and lucrative award (today the award is about $1 million)? If so, what are they?

High and Low

Tibet is the highest country in the world, with an average elevation of over 4,000 meters (12,000 feet). But this high place has had its share of lows. The most recent was in the late 1950s, when an invasion by neighboring China forced Tibet's leader, the Dalai Lama, to flee to another country, where he remains until this day.

Throughout most of its history, Tibet has been a theocracy, which means that its government is made up of religious leaders. In the case of Tibet, these are *lamas*, or monks. The head of Tibet's government is the Dalai Lama (which means "monk with an ocean of wisdom"). Tibet is a Buddhist country, and in Tibetan Buddhism it is generally believed that the Dalai Lama is the reincarnation (rebirth in another body) of Buddha, the founder of Buddhism. The current Dalai Lama is considered the 14th reincarnation of Buddha.

> ◆◆◆**It's a Fact!**◆◆◆
>
> The highest mountain range in the world, the Himalayas, is partially in Tibet. This range includes Mt. Everest, the world's highest point.

Llasa, the capital of Tibet

Tibet is located on a southwest portion of land controlled by China. Since the 18th century, China has controlled Tibet much of the time. Tibet is a much smaller country than China, so there is not much it can do to defend itself. (To give you an idea of how much smaller, think of it this way: China has about 500 times more people than Tibet.) China had sometimes left Tibet pretty much alone, but in 1959 it wanted to reestablish its control of Tibet, replacing Tibet's theocracy with China's communism. Because of this, the Dalai Lama fled to nearby India, as did about 100,000 other Tibetans. The United Nations has criticized China for treating the Tibetan people very badly, but Tibet is still not free. Today there are many people—including famous political figures and entertainers—who work on behalf of the "Free Tibet" movement.

═══ Questions to Ponder ═══

1. What country has given Tibet the most trouble?

2. What kind of government has Tibet usually been?

3. As of 2003, how long had Tibet's leader been living in another country?

4. If China has a population of 1.2 billion, what is Tibet's population?

5. Over the years, many Tibetans have fought the Chinese in an effort to free Tibet—including by using violence, which the Dalai Lama does not approve of. Do you think it is all right for Tibetans to use violence to try to make their country free of Chinese rule? Why or why not?

The Cold War

During World War II, the United States and the Union of Soviet Socialist Republics (U.S.S.R.), although they were not friendly, worked together to help defeat the so-called Axis powers—Germany, Japan, and Italy. However, even before the war ended in 1945, there were many disagreements between the two powerful countries over what post-war Europe would be like. What would happen between the two countries for almost the next half-century came to be known as "the Cold War," a fight between two political philosophies—but a fight in which the two sides would never exchange a single blow.

Since its formation, the U.S. had been a democratic country, which meant that its people got to participate directly in their government and economy. The U.S.S.R. was formed in 1922 by combining Russia and neighboring areas under the philosophy of communism, in which property, resources, and the production of goods were not owned by the individual but by the community—which, on a large scale, meant the government. In the first years after WWII, the U.S.S.R.—which believed communism was a philosophy that would better the world—installed communist governments in Romania, Hungary, Poland, and Bulgaria. The U.S.—which believed democracy was the best philosophy—wanted to keep communism from expanding into other parts of the world, and so it began its policy of "containment," which included aid to anti-Communist forces in a variety of countries. Perhaps the place this conflict was most noticeable was in Germany, which was eventually actually split into two nations—communist East Germany and democratic West Germany. Germany's capital city of Berlin was also split in half, as the Soviets built the Berlin Wall to keep East Germans from leaving. Meanwhile, more countries around the U.S.S.R. began to be taken over by communist governments, and this group of countries and the U.S.S.R. came to be known as the Soviet bloc.

◆◆◆It's a Fact!◆◆◆

The term "the Cold War" comes from the title of a 1947 book by American journalist Walter Lippmann. He felt that, only two years after the end of World War II, relations had become so bad between the U.S.S.R. and its WWII allies that it was like a war without shots being fired.

In the following years, the U.S. and the U.S.S.R. often supported opposite sides of conflicts in many countries, such as the wars in Korea and Vietnam. One of the reasons the U.S. and U.S.S.R. never actually went to war directly with each other is because both countries had nuclear weapons and realized that the world could be destroyed if a war between them got bad enough. Still, one almost happened in 1962, when the U.S. became aware that the U.S.S.R. was putting nuclear missiles in Cuba, a communist country just 90 miles from the U.S. The U.S. blocked Soviet ships off the coast of Cuba with ships of its own—but no shots were fired, and the U.S.S.R. finally agreed to remove its missiles.

Ronald Reagan was elected U.S. president in 1980. He called the U.S.S.R. an "evil empire," believing the only thing it understood was force, and so he began to spend huge sums of money on weapons. The U.S.S.R. was not as wealthy as the U.S., and so, while the U.S. went into debt from spending so much on weapons, the U.S.S.R. began to feel genuine hardship from trying to keep up with the U.S. In 1985, Mikhail Gorbachev became the leader of the U.S.S.R.—and he proved to be the last. Not long after he came to power, he began to change the U.S.S.R. policies, giving more freedom to his people and removing his military from other countries. Reagan and Gorbachev came to like each other personally, and partly because of this, both countries agreed to stop spending so much on weapons and also to reduce the number of nuclear weapons they had.

The Cold War *(cont.)*

Because of the increased freedoms Gorbachev had allowed, many communist governments around the world began to be overthrown. The Berlin Wall was torn down in 1989; and by 1991 the U.S.S.R. no longer existed, instead reverting to Russia and the other individual republics that it had been comprised of. The Cold War was over.

Time Line of the Cold War

- 1917 . . . . . Bolsheviks (later Communists) overthrow Russian government
- 1922 . . . . . U.S.S.R. formed
- 1941 . . . . . U.S.S.R. joins U.S. and its allies to fight Axis powers
- 1942 . . . . . U.S. begins to develop nuclear weapons
- 1945 . . . . . WWII ends; U.S.S.R. establishes communist government in Poland
- 1947 . . . . . U.S. aids anti-Communist forces in Greece and Turkey
- 1949 . . . . . Germany split in two; U.S.S.R. develops nuclear weapons
- 1950–'53 . . Korean War
- 1959–'75 . . Vietnam War
- 1961 . . . . . Berlin Wall built
- 1962 . . . . . Cuban missile crisis
- 1979 . . . . . U.S.S.R. invades Afghanistan, U.S. backs anti-Communist forces
- 1980 . . . . . U.S. boycotts Olympics (held in Moscow, U.S.S.R.) because of U.S.S.R.'s invasion of Afghanistan; Reagan elected U.S. president
- 1984 . . . . . U.S.S.R. boycotts Olympics (held in Los Angeles, U.S.)
- 1985 . . . . . Gorbachev becomes leader of U.S.S.R.
- 1987 . . . . . U.S. and U.S.S.R. first agree to reduce nuclear weapons
- 1989 . . . . . U.S.S.R. withdraws troops from Afghanistan; Berlin Wall is torn down
- 1991 . . . . . U.S.S.R. dissolves

Questions to Ponder

1. Both the U.S. and the U.S.S.R. believed that their own political philosophies were best for the world. What were these two philosophies?

2. The U.S. had a policy to keep communism from spreading throughout the world. What was it called?

3. For how many years did the U.S.S.R. exist?

4. Name five countries where the U.S. and U.S.S.R. backed opposing sides.

5. When Ronald Reagan took office, he believed that building up U.S. military power was the best way to keep the Soviet Union in check. If you had become president when Reagan did, how do you think you might have dealt with the U.S.S.R.?

Science and Technology

The Productive Revolution

When people say, "revolution," usually they are talking about war, violence, and the overthrow of governments. But one revolution—the Industrial Revolution—was about creation, not destruction. This may have been the biggest revolution of all.

Factories have existed at least as far back as the Roman Empire. However, the goods were made by hand, which limited not only the amount that could be made, but also the types. This began to change in the 18th century with inventions in the textile industry (the business of making fabrics). These inventions were basic machines that allowed spinning and weaving (done by hand before) to be done more quickly and cheaply. An even more important invention was James Watt's improved steam engine. Before that, water power (such as a waterwheel on a river) was the only way machines in factories could be powered (aside from by hand)—so these factories could be built only by the water. But the steam engine changed that, and factories now had more power and could be built anywhere. Also, the steam engine led to the steamship and steam locomotive, so goods could be taken farther away to be sold. Another important invention was Henry Bessemer's process for making steel from iron. The greater strength and lighter weight of steel allowed things to be built in ways they had not been before. The tallest buildings and the longest bridges could not have been built without the invention of steel.

The Industrial Revolution changed society from mostly agricultural (people living in the country, on farms, etc.) to more urban, as cities became bigger and people moved to them to work in the large factories being built as technology advanced. People who lived before the Industrial Revolution would not have recognized this new world.

Some Major Milestones of the Industrial Revolution

1712—first commercially-successful steam engine

1775—first efficient steam engine

1779—first steam-powered mills

1786—first efficient steam engine in a cotton mill

1801—steam locomotive

1807—first successful steamboat

1830—growth of commercial railway service in England

1837—telegraph; first ocean-going steamship

1849—reinforced concrete

1850—refining of gasoline

1851—first practical sewing machine

1854—steel

1859—first successful gasoline engine

1867—dynamite

Questions to Ponder

1. Approximately when did the Industrial Revolution begin?
2. Which industry was the first to be affected by the Industrial Revolution?
3. What invention allowed factories to be built in more places than before?
4. How did the Industrial Revolution change where people lived?
5. Between 1811 and 1815, workers in England would often break into factories and destroy machines, fearing that these machines would replace them—which did happen sometimes. How would you feel if you lost your job to a machine? What would you do about it?

Bridging the Gap

Take a log and drop it across a stream, and you've got yourself a bridge. Stretch a rope between two cliffs, you've got yourself another. The basic idea behind bridges is very simple: anything that runs between two points and allows you to travel over something can be said to be a bridge. So, as you might guess, bridges have been around for a long, long time—since before recorded history. But while bridges can be as simple today as they were then, the difference between then and now is technology. What we usually think of as bridges today are somewhat more than just logs and ropes.

Steel is the material used in the building of all of the longest bridges. This is because steel is very strong. Steel has been around for hundreds of years, but it was only in the mid 19th century that we learned to make steel efficiently enough to use it for bridge-building. It is no surprise that the world's longest bridges have been built since then.

There are several ways a bridge can be built. The single type that can be built the longest is the *suspension bridge*, which consists of the supports and the span. The span is the horizontal part that crosses a valley or river; and the supports are the towers that hold the span up. Large cables are stretched between the tops of the towers, and many smaller cables hang down from these to the span, giving it support—in other words, suspending it. A longer type of bridge is the *combination bridge*, but, as the name tells you, this is not a single bridge but a combination of bridges of different types. The longest one in the world is Lake Pontchartrain in Louisiana, U.S., which measures 38,600 meters in length.

World's 10 Longest Bridges*

Bridge	Type	Country	Year	Length (meters)
Akashi Kaikyo	suspension	Japan	1998	1991
Great Belt Bridge	suspension	Denmark	1998	1624
Humber	suspension	Great Britain	1981	1410
Jiangyin	suspension	China	1998	1385
Tsing Ma	suspension	Hong Kong	1997	1377
Verrazano-Narrows	suspension	U.S.	1964	1298
Golden Gate	suspension	U.S.	1937	1280
Höga Kusten	suspension	Sweden	1997	1210
Mackinac	suspension	U.S.	1957	1158
Minami Bisan-Seto	suspension	Japan	1988	1100

*does not include combination bridges

Questions to Ponder

1. What is the longest single type of bridge?

2. What is the name of the part of a bridge across which people can walk and/or cars can drive?

3. In which decade were most of the world's 10 longest bridges built? What percentage of them were built then?

4. How many of the world's very longest suspension bridge (the Akashi Kaikyo) would you have to put together until you ended up with something longer than the world's longest combination bridge?

5. Although bridges have been around for thousands of years, the use of steel has allowed bridges to be built longer than ever before. What is another type of structure that steel has allowed to be built longer, bigger, or higher than it could have been before? Why do you think this is?

Turning Water into Electricity

Water has been harnessed as a source of energy at least as far back as ancient Greece, when waterwheels were used for milling corn. However, it was not until the 20th century, when advancements were made in construction, machinery, and our understanding of electricity, that water could be used to power entire cities. This was achieved through creation of the hydroelectric dam.

Dams were being built as early as 4000 B.C., so both the ideas of the dam and of using water to generate energy are very old. The first hydroelectric dam was built in 1882 in Appleton, Wisconsin. This was only three years after the invention of the light bulb, so obviously the connection between waterpower and how it related to generating electricity was easy to make. In that sense, there is nothing complicated about the hydroelectric dam. Basically, all that a hydroelectric dam does is (1) impound (or *hold back*) the flow of water in a river, (2) let a controlled amount of water flow through certain tunnels, where it (3) turns turbines (motors that are turned in much the same manner as waterwheels) that are connected to generators, which (4) turn that motion into electricity, which is then (5) transmitted along power lines.

This relatively simple idea has changed the world. Today, hydroelectric dams exist in 150 countries around the world and are responsible for about 20% of the world's total electricity. Twenty-four countries get 90% of their electricity this way. The largest dam in the world produces enough energy to light 120 million 100-watt bulbs at one time. While hydroelectric dams are a clean source of natural energy, the nearby ecosystem is affected when the dams are built. When the 770-foot high Hoover Dam was built on the Colorado River in 1936, it created Lake Mead, a body of water taking up 247 square miles of what once had been dry land.

World's Most Powerful Hydroelectric Power Plants

Name of Dam	Location	Output (in megawatts)	Began Operating
1. Itaipu	Brazil/Paraguay	12,600	1983
2. Guri	Venezuela	10,000	1986
3. Grand Coulee	Washington, U.S.	6,494	1942
4. Sayano-Shushensk	Russia	6,400	1989
5. Krasnoyarsk	Russia	6,000	1968
6. Churchill Falls	Canada	5,428	1971
7. La Grande 2	Canada	5,328	1979
8. Bratsk	Russia	4,500	1961
9. Moxoto	Brazil	4,328	not available
10. Ust-Ilim	Russia	4,320	1977

Questions to Ponder

1. When and where was the first hydroelectric dam built?

2. What advancements were needed to go from the building of the earliest dams to the building of hydroelectric dams?

3. Which country has the largest number of the ten most powerful dams?

4. What percentage of countries with hydroelectric dams get 90% of their electricity this way?

5. In what ways do you think the building of a hydroelectric dam might affect an area's ecosystem?

How Film Came to Be

Today, movies are produced all the time. Many of us have a video or digital camera, so we can make our own sorts of film. Because of this, it's easy to forget that recording moving images is not simple at all but something that required many individual advances in technology.

As we know it today, film is a combination of many things. The first is the recording of a still image. Life is not still, of course, so the next step was to find a way to record motion. Once this had been achieved, it was necessary to project the image. When this task had been mastered, attention was turned to sound—because life isn't silent, after all. The first need was to synchronize sound with the film image. However, this is different from just recording sound that is in front of the camera. It called for a new technology. Then came the problem of color images, since early photography produced only differences in light and dark (or what we call "black and white" images). But all of this is beyond some of the basic inventions needed to make any of it possible. For example, since light is an essential element of filmmaking, none of it would exist if the light bulb had not been invented first. This is true of many inventions: they would not exist if not for a great many that had come before.

✦✦✦It's a Fact!✦✦✦

The term "movie" is actually a nickname for "motion picture"—a moving image, or "movie." Movies are actually a series of still pictures that succeed each other very rapidly, giving the illusion of motion—just like animation. The standard rate used today is 24 frames (or still pictures) per second.

Selected Inventions That Led to What Film Is Today

Invention	Inventor(s)	What It Did	Date
thaumatrope	John A. Paris	created illusion of moving images by using still ones	1826
camera	William H.F. Talbot	captured pictures of objects	1851
kinetoscope	Dickson, Thomas Edison	displayed moving image (for one person)	1889
kinetograph	William K.L. Dickson	filmed moving images	1890
cinématographe	Lumière Bros.	first efficient and portable movie camera	1895
vitascope	Edison, Thomas Armat	projected a moving image	1896
chronophone	Leon Gaumont	joined sound and image together for projection	1902
autochrome process	Lumière Bros.	produced colored film images	1904
audion	Lee de Forest	electronic tube used for amplification of sound	1907
"talkies"	Warner Bros.	allowed on-camera dialog to be heard	1927

Questions to Ponder

1. What does "illusion" mean?
2. Which is the first invention above that concerned sound, and when was it invented?
3. The word "scope" is used in more than one of the inventions above. What do you think it means?
4. Other than film cameras, what two other types of cameras are used today?
5. Without the light bulb, there could never have been the movies. What are some other things you can think of that are not listed above that had to be invented before motion pictures could exist? Explain your answers.

The Most Famous Scientist

Say to a friend, "You're a Darwin," and that friend will probably be confused; call the person a Newton, and the friend may think you're talking about a cookie; but if you call anyone an Einstein, that person is bound to know exactly what you mean. This is because the brilliant Albert Einstein is the one scientist whom just about everyone has heard of. But why?

Einstein was born in Germany on March 14, 1879. He did not speak until he was three years old, but at an early age he displayed a great understanding of math and the natural world. Although he did not particularly enjoy school, by 12 he had taught himself Euclidean geometry. Eventually he did earn his middle-school and college degrees, and at 23 he was working as a patent clerk in Switzerland. In 1905 he received his doctorate—but, more importantly, that was the year he published three papers that would change the face of science forever. Included in one of these papers is the theory of relativity, which gives us the world's most famous math equation, $E = mc^2$. To put it simply, this means that energy (like electricity or sunlight) and matter (like a desk or you) are really the same thing. Among the many other things Einstein showed the world is that time is relative to the observer (i.e., the person making the measurement), and that gravity is the curving of space. His ideas were so revolutionary that many of his fellow scientists were very slow to comprehend them. Eventually, it was seen that Einstein was right, and he was awarded the Nobel Prize in Physics in 1921.

> ◇◇◇**It's a Fact!**◇◇◇
>
> Einstein was so respected that, although he never expressed an interest in being a politician, he was offered the chance to be the president of Israel in 1952. He declined.

Einstein, who was born Jewish (although he was not religious), lived the last third of his life in the United States, having fled Germany once Adolf Hitler and his Nazi Party came to power. Einstein used his fame to promote peace, freedom, and the cause of the Jewish people. He died on April 15, 1955, but his reputation as perhaps the greatest scientific mind in history has only grown since that time.

Questions to Ponder

1. If someone calls you an Einstein, what are they saying about you?

2. How old was Einstein at the time of his death?

3. What does "revolutionary" mean?

4. Basically, what does $E = mc^2$ mean?

5. Einstein valued peace, freedom, and thinking more than anything else. What do you think Einstein would think of the world today? Explain your answer, addressing these three things.

Albert Einstein

The Computer Age

We are living in the Computer Age, as computers are major parts of almost every aspect of life. Computers are so commonplace that it may be hard to believe that prior to only about 30 years ago almost no one in the world had a personal computer at home.

Many of the basic ideas about the computer were thought up in the 1830s by Charles Babbage—although the technology of his day was not advanced enough for him to build it. If it had been, it would have been the size of a football field and taken the power of five steam engines to operate! But even when technology caught up and surpassed Babbage's ideas, the first true computers took up entire rooms. It was with the inventions of the transistor (which allowed for controlling the flow of an electrical current as never before) and then the integrated circuit (which is the same size as a transistor but can do the work of 20), that computers began to be made smaller and smaller. This led to the development of the microprocessor, which is a computer's entire central processing unit (CPU) contained on a single chip. By 1975 things had become small enough that the first personal computers (PCs) were being sold. By the '80s computers continued to get smaller, more powerful, and cheaper to make, and so they became much easier to buy. Think of how things have changed: in 1972, no personal computers had been sold; 30 years later, that number had reached about 1 billion.

To give you an idea of how much smaller things have become in the computer industry, imagine this: although today's microprocessor is about the size of a postage stamp, it can contain up to *10 million* transistors—in addition to other parts! And size isn't the only improvement, as an average personal computer today is faster and has more power than the computers used by NASA in 1969 to put the first man on the moon.

Selected Computer Milestones

What	Who	When
first mechanical calculator	Wilhelm Schikard	1623
first program (punch cards for a loom)	Joseph Marie Jacquard	1790
electrical punch-card tabulating system	Herman Hollerith	1889
first fully functional digital computer	Konrad Zuse	1941
transistor	W.H. Brattain, J. Bardeen, & W.B. Shockley	1948
integrated circuit	Jack Kilby & Robert Noyce	1958
microprocessor	Intel	1971
first widely-marketed personal computer	MITS	1975
first PC word-processing program	Michael Shrayer	1976
first PC with color graphics	Apple Computer	1977
first PC with GUI and mouse	Apple Computer	1984

Questions to Ponder

1. Who first came up with many of the basic ideas of the modern computer?

2. From the article above, you can see that as computer technology has advanced, computers have gotten _____. (*Fill in the blank.*)

3. How long was it between the development of the first program of any sort and the first word-processing program for PCs?

4. As of 2002, about how many PCs had been sold?

5. Personal computers were non-existent about 30 years ago. How do you think the PCs of 30 years from now will differ from the ones of today?

Harnessing the Atom

The majority of the energy harnessed in modern societies comes from the burning of fossil fuels—coal, natural gas, and petroleum. There are two major problems with these forms of energy: since they are burned, they create air pollution; and there is a limited amount of them on the planet—thus, they will eventually run out. Other forms of energy are things like solar and wind power, but we do not yet know how to generate a great deal of energy in this way. One form of energy different from both these is nuclear energy.

The term "nuclear" refers to the nucleus of the atom ("atomic energy" is just another term for nuclear energy). Nuclear energy can be generated by a process called fission, which is the splitting of the nuclei of certain radioactive elements. When these nuclei are split, the reaction produces a tremendous amount of energy. Unlike fossil fuels, fissionable material is plentiful, chiefly because so much energy can be developed from so little material. Also, since the energy is not produced by burning, there is no air pollution. The main drawback is that there is leftover material from the fission process, called radioactive waste, that is dangerous and must be dealt with very carefully.

Nuclear power plants have been operating since the 1940s, and many countries now obtain a significant percentage of their energy this way. Also, small-scale nuclear reactors are sometimes used to power military vehicles such as submarines. Nuclear-powered vehicles rarely run out of fuel, since they can run for so long with so little because of the intense energy generated in a nuclear reaction.

The future of nuclear power will come from a process called fusion, in which two atoms are combined instead of one being split. This is how stars generate their energy. The advantages of fusion are three-fold: (1) material for fusion is easy to get, as it can be drawn from the ocean; (2) there is no chance of an accident happening at a reactor; and (3) much less waste is generated, and it is not so dangerous.

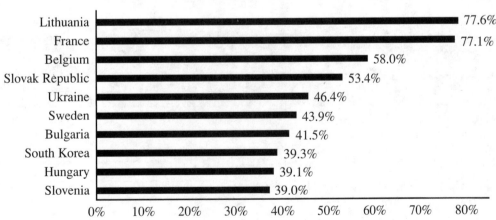

Nations Most Reliant on Nuclear Energy, 2001

Nation	Percentage
Lithuania	77.6%
France	77.1%
Belgium	58.0%
Slovak Republic	53.4%
Ukraine	46.4%
Sweden	43.9%
Bulgaria	41.5%
South Korea	39.3%
Hungary	39.1%
Slovenia	39.0%

Questions to Ponder

1. What is the main advantage of nuclear power?

2. What are the two kinds of nuclear energy, and how do they differ?

3. What does the word "drawback" mean?

4. How many countries in the world get at least 2/5 of their power from nuclear power plants?

5. Do you think it is better to be reliant on nuclear power or on fossil fuels? Explain your answer.

Living Longer

It's simple: people are living longer. The reasons for this, though, are complex. They have to do with the world and the changes we have made to it—and to our own lives.

In ancient times people did not live as long as they do now, but because we do not have complete records of those times, we don't have a great deal of specific information about how long people lived—but we do have some. In the Roman Empire, for example, an individual's life expectancy at birth (the average lifespan of all people born—averaging together all those who died at one month old, those who lived to be 80, and everybody else) was only 25 years—chiefly because so many children died in infancy. Things didn't change much for thousands of years. As recently as 1900, the news was not much better: the average child born that year had a life expectancy of 30 years. However, the average life expectancy of someone born today is about 62 years! What happened over the last century to account for such an extreme change?

The answer is knowledge and technology. Our understanding of things has increased dramatically since 1900. For example, a hundred years ago we still knew relatively little about diseases—and even less about how to treat and prevent them. Today we know how to avoid many diseases, we know how to treat others, and we have even been able to eliminate a few. We also know much more about nutrition and how to care for infants and the elderly, we have better methods for growing food and keeping it safe, and we have improved our overall living conditions. Generally, the more technologically advanced a society is, the longer its people can expect to live. This explains why babies born in the U.S. (one of the most technologically-advanced countries in the world) have a life expectancy of 77 years—or 15 years longer than the world average. In short, our understanding of our world and our ability to make it better has allowed us to live much longer than we did at any other time in history.

Life Expectancy at Birth in the U.S., 1900–2000

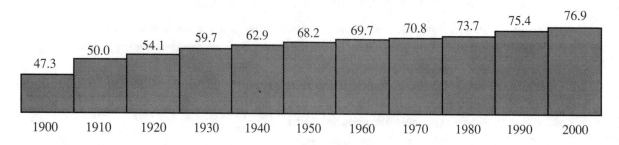

1900	1910	1920	1930	1940	1950	1960	1970	1980	1990	2000
47.3	50.0	54.1	59.7	62.9	68.2	69.7	70.8	73.7	75.4	76.9

Questions to Ponder

1. Approximately how much longer is the life expectancy of someone born in the world today than it was for someone born in 1900?

2. As a percentage, how much longer could people born in the U.S. in 2000 expect to live than people born in ancient Rome?

3. What are the main reasons people live so much longer today than they did just a century ago?

4. What does "eliminate" mean?

5. Many countries today which are not technologically advanced have a high infant-mortality rate (a high percentage of babies do not survive)—just as it was in the Roman Empire. Why do you think a lack of technology particularly affects a baby's chances of survival?

The Net Around the World

"Internet" is a shortened version of "interconnected network," and that's exactly what it is: a system of computers connected to each other. Small groups of interconnected computers are called internets, and the Internet is the interconnection of all of these. If you access the Internet, your computer is potentially interacting with millions of others.

The idea for the Internet came about in the late 1960s. The U.S. military wanted a way of connecting computers in such a way that if anything went wrong with one part of the network, the other parts would still be able to interact with each other. The first version was called ARPANET, and in 1969 it connected just four computers with one another. By 1971 it had grown to about a couple dozen. Ten years later it had grown to about 200, but only the military and people doing research at certain universities had access to it.

Over the coming years the technology was improved, but it was the invention of the World Wide Web (WWW) by scientist Tim Berners-Lee in 1989 that turned the Internet into what we know today. If you imagine the Internet as a single computer, the WWW is like a program that allows you access to all of the different things your computer can do—without your need to be a computer specialist. The first browser (software that allows one to easily navigate the WWW) was released in 1991, and the Internet started to grow at an amazing rate. By 1994, about 3 million people in the world had access to the Internet; but by 2002, about 166 million in the U.S. alone were online. As far as the Internet itself, no one really knows how big it is now. The closest guess is that hundreds of billions of pages can be accessed. Most of those pages are available to anyone with a computer. The Internet belongs to no one and to everyone; so all who wish may not only access the Internet, but they can also add to it—add anything they want.

The Internet's Major Historical Highlights

- 1969 . . . . ARPANET established by Advanced Research Projects Agency (ARPA) of the U.S. Defense Dept.
- 1971 . . . . ARPANET consists of about two dozen computers.
- 1981 . . . . ARPANET consists of about 200 computers.
- 1983 . . . . Military portion of ARPANET moved to MILNET.
- late '80s . . . . National Science Foundation launches NSFNET, which anyone can get on and use.
- 1988 . . . . Internet Relay Chat (IRC) invented, which allowed people to communicate in real time.
- 1989 . . . . The World, the first commercial Internet access service, is made available.
- 1989–'90 . . . . World Wide Web (WWW) is invented.
- 1991 . . . . First WWW browser is released.
- 1993 . . . . First WWW browser with graphics is released.

Questions to Ponder

1. What was the name of the first version of the Internet?

2. Who invented the World Wide Web?

3. How long was it between the development of the beginnings of the Internet and the establishment of the first commercial Internet service?

4. As of 2002, how many times more Americans had Internet access than there were people in the entire world that had it just eight years earlier?

5. Do you like the Internet being controlled by no one, or do you think it would be better if there were someone watching over it? Explain your answer.

Eye in the Sky

Although not understood when Galileo was looking at the sky, a problem with all Earth-based telescopes is that they look through our planet's atmosphere to view the heavens. Much in our air gets in the way of a clear view of what's out there, from simple things like dust and smoke to things like small variations in temperature (which makes the stars look as if they twinkle—even though they really don't!). As this became better understood, astronomers realized the best way to look into space was to put a telescope out there—that is, in orbit around Earth, outside of its atmosphere.

✧✧✧It's a Fact!✧✧✧

The HST is named for astronomer Edwin Hubble (1889–1953), best-known for his realization that the universe is inflationary, or expanding— the result of what most of us call "the Big Bang."

Work began on the Hubble Space Telescope (HST) in 1977. The telescope itself was completed in 1985, and five years later it was put into orbit. Unlike earlier orbital telescopes, the HST was the first that could record actual optical images. Immediately it provided us with some of the best images of space ever recorded. However, NASA scientists noted a problem with the telescope's primary mirror that kept the images from being better. Because of this, many people felt the $3 billion project was a failure. But in 1993 a successful service mission was carried out, after which everyone agreed that the HST lived up to its promise. With powerful technology, the HST has provided scientists with thousands of breathtaking images and other important data, such as the first direct evidence of black holes and the first image of a planet outside our solar system.

Steps to the HST—a Time Line

1608	Hans Lipperhey credited with inventing first telescope
1609	Galileo uses homemade telescope to look into the sky
1668	Isaac Newton builds first reflecting telescope (i.e., first one to use a mirror)
mid 1800s	photography first used to record telescopic images
1920s	first ideas about putting a telescope into orbit
1930s	radio telescopes are first developed
1957	first man-made satellite, *Sputnik 1*
early 1960s	infrared, ultraviolet, and X-ray telescopes are first developed
1977	HST project begins
1985	HST completed
1990	HST put into orbit
1993	problem with HST fixed
late 1990s	series of HST upgrades made
2010	projected end of HST mission

Questions to Ponder

1. How many years elapsed between the invention of the first telescope and the completion of the HST?

2. Who built the first telescope that used a mirror, and when was it built?

3. What was wrong with the HST when it first went into orbit? How much had been spent on the HST to that point?

4. What does "transparent" mean?

5. What is something about the universe that you'd like to know? Do you think anyone knows or will ever know the answer to your question? Elaborate.

The Natural World

The Building Blocks
of Everything

WORLD ALMANAC

Elements are made up of atoms, which are made up of protons, neutrons, and electrons—which, in turn, are made up of even smaller particles. However, in day-to-day life, you will not encounter anything more basic than the elements. Everything you see, touch, taste, or even breathe is made up of the elements.

The elements are broken down into two categories: metals and non-metals. Examples of metals are iron (Fe), copper (Cu), and aluminum (Al); while examples of non-metals are hydrogen (H), helium (He), and oxygen (O). Elements are types of atoms—for example, hydrogen (the most common element in the universe) is hydrogen atoms. These atoms can bond together with each other, and most also bond in certain combinations with some other types of atoms. A couple of well-known examples of this are water, which is the combination of two hydrogen atoms with one oxygen atom (dihydrous oxide, or H_2O), and salt, which is the bonding together of one sodium and one chlorine atom (sodium chloride, or NaCl).

◇◇◇It's a Fact!◇◇◇

Not all of the elements on the periodic table seem to exist naturally in the universe. These are the *transuranium elements*, and they are all man-made. The first of these was rutherfordium (Rf), first created in 1964.

You may be at least somewhat familiar with the periodic table of elements. This was developed by Russian chemist Dmitry Mendeleyev. About half of the elements were known by then, but no one had been able to see any order. What scientists did see was that certain elements seemed to be naturally organized in groups that had similar types of chemical reactions. For example, they knew that lithium (Li), sodium (Na), and potassium (K) combined with other elements in pretty much the same way. What Mendeleyev saw while trying to group the elements together for a textbook he was writing was that, when you put all of the elements together, there is an overall pattern. In 1871 he published an improved version of his first periodic table, leaving blank spaces on this one where he believed there must be other elements to fill out these patterns. His table began to become accepted in 1879 when scandium (Sc) was discovered to fill exactly the blank space that Mendeleyev had left between calcium (Ca) and titanium (Ti).

Atoms are made up of three parts: protons and neutrons, which group together at the center of the atom to form its nucleus; and electrons, which move around the nucleus at different levels. It was later understood that the pattern of the elements is caused by the number of electrons in an atom, because each of these electron levels can have only a certain number of electrons in it. It is the space for other electrons that allows atoms to combine with other atoms—and that is why some kinds of elements act like other elements: because their electrons are laid out in the same way. You can see this on the periodic table by looking at the vertical columns. Notice how the numbers in the columns increase by the same amounts? Those numbers are how many electrons those atoms have. That's why these numbers are called the elements' *atomic numbers*.

The Building Blocks of Everything *(cont.)*

Periodic Table of the Elements

Source: © 1996 Lawrence Berkeley National Laboratory

Parentheses indicate undiscovered elements.

Key example:
- atomic number: 14
- atomic weight: 28.09
- symbol: Si
- name: Silicon

Group labels: alkali metals · alkaline earth metals · transitional metals · other metals · nonmetals · noble gases

1 (alkali)	2 (alkaline earth)	3–12 (transitional metals)										13	14	15	16	17	18 (noble gases)
1 **H** 1.01 Hydrogen																	2 **He** 4.003 Helium
3 **Li** 6.94 Lithium	4 **Be** 9.01 Beryllium											5 **B** 10.81 Boron	6 **C** 12.01 Carbon	7 **N** 14.01 Nitrogen	8 **O** 15.999 Oxygen	9 **F** 18.998 Fluorine	10 **Ne** 20.18 Neon
11 **Na** 22.99 Sodium	12 **Mg** 24.31 Magnesium											13 **Al** 26.98 Aluminum	14 **Si** 28.09 Silicon	15 **P** 30.97 Phosphorus	16 **S** 32.06 Sulfur	17 **Cl** 35.45 Chlorine	18 **Ar** 39.95 Argon
19 **K** 39.10 Potassium	20 **Ca** 40.08 Calcium	21 **Sc** 44.96 Scandium	22 **Ti** 47.90 Titanium	23 **V** 50.94 Vanadium	24 **Cr** 51.996 Chromium	25 **Mn** 54.94 Manganese	26 **Fe** 55.85 Iron	27 **Co** 58.93 Cobalt	28 **Ni** 58.70 Nickel	29 **Cu** 63.55 Copper	30 **Zn** 65.37 Zinc	31 **Ga** 69.72 Gallium	32 **Ge** 72.59 Germanium	33 **As** 74.92 Arsenic	34 **Se** 78.96 Selenium	35 **Br** 79.90 Bromine	36 **Kr** 83.80 Krypton
37 **Rb** 85.47 Rubidium	38 **Sr** 87.62 Strontium	39 **Y** 88.91 Yttrium	40 **Zr** 91.22 Zirconium	41 **Nb** 92.91 Niobium	42 **Mo** 95.94 Molybdenum	43 **Tc** 98 Technetium	44 **Ru** 101.07 Ruthenium	45 **Rh** 102.91 Rhodium	46 **Pd** 106.40 Palladium	47 **Ag** 107.87 Silver	48 **Cd** 112.41 Cadmium	49 **In** 114.82 Indium	50 **Sn** 118.69 Tin	51 **Sb** 121.75 Antimony	52 **Te** 127.60 Tellurium	53 **I** 126.90 Iodine	54 **Xe** 131.30 Xenon
55 **Cs** 132.91 Cesium	56 **Ba** 137.33 Barium	57 **La** 138.91 Lanthanum	72 **Hf** 178.49 Hafnium	73 **Ta** 180.95 Tantalum	74 **W** 183.85 Tungsten	75 **Re** 186.21 Rhenium	76 **Os** 190.20 Osmium	77 **Ir** 192.22 Iridium	78 **Pt** 195.09 Platinum	79 **Au** 196.97 Gold	80 **Hg** 200.59 Mercury	81 **Tl** 204.37 Thallium	82 **Pb** 207.19 Lead	83 **Bi** 208.98 Bismuth	84 **Po** 209 Polonium	85 **At** 210 Astatine	86 **Rn** 222 Radon
87 **Fr** 223 Francium	88 **Ra** 226.03 Radium	89 **Ac** 227.03 Actinium	104 **Rf** 261 Rutherfordium	105 **Ha/Db** 262 Hahnium/Dubnium	106 **Sg** 263 Seaborgium	107 **Bh** 262 Bohrium	108 **Hs** 265 Hassium	109 **Mt** 266 Meitnerium	110 267	111 272	112 277	(113)	(114)	(115)	(116)	(117)	(118)

Lanthanide series:

58 **Ce** 140.12 Cerium	59 **Pr** 140.91 Praseodymium	60 **Nd** 144.24 Neodymium	61 **Pm** 145 Promethium	62 **Sm** 150.35 Samarium	63 **Eu** 151.96 Europium	64 **Gd** 157.25 Gadolinium	65 **Tb** 158.93 Terbium	66 **Dy** 162.50 Dysprosium	67 **Ho** 164.93 Holmium	68 **Er** 167.26 Erbium	69 **Tm** 168.93 Thulium	70 **Yb** 173.04 Ytterbium	71 **Lu** 174.97 Lutetium

Actinide series:

90 **Th** 232.04 Thorium	91 **Pa** 231.04 Protactinium	92 **U** 238.03 Uranium	93 **Np** 237.05 Neptunium	94 **Pu** 238.03 Plutonium	95 **Am** 243 Americium	96 **Cm** 247 Curium	97 **Bk** 247 Berkelium	98 **Cf** 251 Californium	99 **Es** 252 Einsteinium	100 **Fm** 257 Fermium	101 **Md** 258 Mendelevium	102 **No** 259 Nobelium	103 **Lr** 262 Lawrencium

Questions to Ponder

1. What type of atoms is oxygen made up of?

2. In what century was the periodic table created?

3. We breathe in oxygen and breathe out carbon dioxide. What is the atomic make-up of carbon dioxide?

4. As you can see, on the periodic table there are blank spaces for elements 113–118, which are labeled "undiscovered elements." How can scientists be sure that elements go here if they haven't discovered them?

5. Look around you. Does it surprise you that everything—this paper and ink, what you ate for breakfast and what you're breathing now, your teacher and your eyes—is made up of fewer than 120 basic elements? Explain why it does or doesn't.

Not *the* Solar System, Just Ours

When people say "the solar system," we all know what they're talking about: Earth and eight other planets orbiting the sun. However, just as our Milky Way galaxy is only one of billions, so too our solar system is only one among billions. For a long time, astronomers have felt this must be the case, but it is only recently that they have found direct evidence of other planets and solar systems. And even though our solar system is not unique, it does give us an up-close example of what an average solar system is like.

Many people think of stars—such as our sun—as things very different from planets, but the truth is that they form in pretty much the same way. What happens is this: a vast cloud of swirling dust and gas (comprised of many different elements) gradually compresses due to gravity. The majority of the material condenses in the center of the cloud, and this becomes a star. The leftover material comes together in little groups in a similar fashion. However, none of these groupings has the mass necessary to become a star, and so they become planets instead. There are two basic types of planets: rocky and gaseous. What accounts for the difference is how close a planet is to the sun: the closer ones are rocky (for example, Mercury, Venus, Earth, Mars) while the farther ones are gaseous (Jupiter, Saturn, Uranus, Neptune).

One thing that may make our solar system a little uncommon is Pluto. Although it is usually the planet farthest from the sun, it is a rocky planet, like Earth. How can this be? Astronomers believe that Pluto is really nothing more than a big asteroid that was floating through space before it became caught in the sun's gravity. Because of this, some astronomers do not consider Pluto a "true" planet!

Our Solar System

Body	Diameter	Atmosphere	Avg. Dist. fr. Sun	Natural Satellites
Sun	1,390,000 km	all gas, mostly H and He	N.A.	9 (the planets)
Mercury	4,879 km	no	57.9 mil km	0
Venus	12,104 km	mostly CO_2	108.2 mil km	0
Earth	12,756 km	78% N, 21% O	149.6 mil km	1
Mars	6,794 km	CO_2	228 mil km	2
Jupiter	142,984 km*	90% H_2	778 mil km	39
Saturn	120,536 km*	75% H, 25% He	1.43 bil km	30
Uranus	51,118 km**	83% H**	2.9 bil km	21
Neptune	49,528 km**	80% H**	4.5 bil km	8
Pluto	2,290 km	no	4.7–7.4 bil km	1

* The surfaces of these planets are completely liquid.

**It is believed that neither of these planets has a true surface, and so diameter estimates are based on where the atmospheric density is in line with Earth's at sea level.

Questions to Ponder

1. What does "solar" mean?

2. How many total moons are there orbiting the nine planets in our solar system?

3. What element seems to be most common in our solar system?

4. Which two planets are closest in size?

5. If there are billions of solar systems like ours, do you think there is life in some of them? Why or why not?

It's About Where on Earth You Are

"Cold climate," "warm climate," "tropical climate"—we hear these terms all the time, and we have no trouble understanding that all they refer to is the general type of weather you find in a place. What the terms don't tell us is why the weather is however it is—why a climate is cold or warm, why it's freezing on Mt. Everest but broiling in the Sahara Desert.

There are four main factors that determine the climate of a given area, and all of them have to do with location. One is the latitude of a place, or how far north or south of the equator a place is. Remember, Earth is a giant, spinning globe that is circling around the sun, Earth's main heat source. Earth's equator is the horizontal zone going around the middle of the globe, and this is the part that is the closest to the sun—and so it is the hottest! The areas at the top and bottom of the globe, the poles, are generally the farthest from the sun, and they never really get any closer as Earth spins. This is why they are the coldest points on Earth, and why they stay that way all year round. (The English word *climate* comes from the Greek *klima*, which means "inclination [angle] of the sun.")

Another factor is elevation, or how high above sea level a place is. At first you might think the higher an area it is, the hotter it would be, since higher areas are closer to the sun. However, the highest places on Earth aren't even 10 miles high, and 10 miles isn't enough to make a difference in terms of getting heat from the sun. (Contrast this with the difference between the equator and the poles, the equator being about 4,000 miles closer to the sun and receives a lot more direct sunlight.) Where elevation does make a difference is in terms of the atmosphere and the way warmer and colder air move within it. This is why the general rule is: the higher the elevation, the colder it is. (So, as you might expect, if you were to get in a balloon and float 30 miles up, you would find it to be colder than any place on Earth.)

A third factor is where a place is in terms of the natural air and ocean currents in that area. Air and water on Earth move at different speeds in different places, and this affects the weather—which, over the long term, affects the climate. These currents are also affected by the rotation of the Earth. The fourth factor is the geographical features of a place—whether it is by the ocean, in a valley, etc. For example, different geographic features influence how the air moves, and how the air moves affects the climate—which affects the plant life, which affects the water cycle, which affects the land, which affects the climate, etc.

Questions to Ponder

1. What is the key to an area's climate?

2. Which is closest to the sun at noon in each of these areas: a beach on the equator, the top of highest mountain on Antarctica, or a cloud high above the North Pole?

3. How does the English word *climate* relate to the definition of the Greek word *klima*?

4. The Earth spins east. Would the climate at the North Pole be different if Earth spun south? Why or why not?

5. What kind of climate would you most like to live in? Describe where on Earth you would expect to find such a climate and what its geographical features would be like.

Waves of Energy

Nearly everyone has heard of radiation, but most know it only as something dangerous, something caused by atomic bomb explosions or nuclear power plant accidents, both of which are extremely rare. However, radiation is a common, necessary thing—something all around you and that you use all the time. Have you cooked something in a microwave oven? Have you listened to the radio or watched TV? Have you seen colors or felt the warmth of the sun? Every one of these things has to do with radiation.

> ❖❖❖**It's a Fact!**❖❖❖
>
> The word "radiation" comes from the root verb "radiate," which means to emit or give off (from a center).

As you can see, radiation appears in many different ways—but all are types of radiation because they are all basically the same thing: waves of energy. What accounts for the different forms this energy seems to take is basically nothing more than how long these waves are, their *wavelengths*. When the waves of energy are very long, they are what we call radio waves. These are the ones by which not just radio but also television signals are transmitted. Radio waves are generally between 1 m and 1 km in length. When the waves are much shorter, they are X-rays—the rays which are used to see through things, like a part of your body at the doctor's office or your luggage at an airport security point. Shorter than radio waves but longer than X-rays are other kinds of radiation, including the kind we can see: visible light. Even within this single form of radiation, differences in wavelengths are noteworthy, as this is what accounts for the different colors we see.

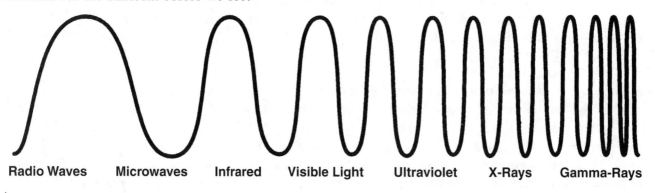

Radio Waves   Microwaves   Infrared   Visible Light   Ultraviolet   X-Rays   Gamma-Rays

* not to scale

Questions to Ponder

1. Which type of wave is the longest? Which is the shortest?

2. We can't see radio waves or X-rays. Are all forms of radiation invisible?

3. The prefix "infra" means *beneath*, and the prefix "ultra" means *beyond*. How does this information apply to the chart above?

4. As you can see from a bottle of sunscreen, sunburn is caused by something called UV rays. What are UV rays and what can you tell about them from the information given above?

5. What kind of radiation do you think affects your life the most? Why?

Space Is Curved

Since before recorded history, people knew that solid objects fell towards Earth, but their ideas about why weren't too developed. In fact, the first major breakthrough in our understanding of this phenomenon didn't come until the beginning of the 17th century, when Galileo realized that all objects—no matter their differing sizes and weights—fall towards Earth at the same rate if you can remove all other factors, such as how air resistance causes a feather to fall more slowly than something like a rock. By the late 17th century, Isaac Newton had realized that gravity was a force that all objects exerted upon all other objects, and that gravity was responsible not only for objects falling towards Earth but also why the planets stay in orbit around the sun. His ideas were so good that it wasn't until the 20th century and Albert Einstein that it was shown that gravity was actually something very different from what Newton had imagined.

According to Einstein, the mass of an object (that is to say, the amount of matter an object is composed of) affects the space around it by actually curving it. Objects with relatively little mass—like a person or a car—have very little effect on space; but more massive objects—like Earth—curve space to a greater degree. Objects fall towards Earth because Earth curves the space around it towards its center—and so this is the direction that objects naturally want to go! Many scientists didn't believe in Einstein's idea, but a solar

> ✦✦✦**It's a Fact!**✦✦✦
>
> The branch of mathematics called *calculus* was invented by Isaac Newton to help him work out his theory of gravity.

eclipse in 1919 gave the world a chance to see that Einstein was right, as scientists were able to observe the space being bent around the sun by seeing that the light from a distant star was not quite where they expected it to be but exactly where Einstein said it would be. Because the space around the sun was curved by the sun's mass, the light appeared to be bent towards the sun as it came by it on its way to Earth.

A simple way to get the basic idea of what mass does to space is stretch a bedsheet taut. Then roll a basketball onto the middle of the sheet. See how the shape of the sheet has been changed by the weight of the ball? This is like what mass does to space—except that it does this in three dimensions, while our experiment gives you an idea of only two.

Questions to Ponder

1. What did Newton call the force that kept the planets orbiting around the sun?

2. What did Einstein realize about gravity?

3. What does "breakthrough" mean?

4. If you were to get in a rocket ship and fly away from Earth (and not near any other massive objects), what would happen to the force of gravity you would feel as you got farther away? Why is this?

5. Pretend gravity somehow suddenly ceased to exist. Explain what you think would happen to our solar system—including what would happen here on Earth.

Fire: What Is It?

Strike a match, flick a lighter—fire, no problem. But what is this thing that we take so much for granted? First, fire is a combination of light and heat. Both of these are the product of the atoms that make up a combustible substance (something that can be lit on fire) being made to move so fast that some start to break away from each other—in other words, heating it up past a certain point (which varies, depending on the substance). This must be done in the presence of oxygen (or sometimes chlorine gas) in order for the substance (in other words, the fuel) to maintain its combustion.

People can make fire in three ways: (1) by friction, in which two objects are rubbed together so that enough heat is generated to ignite nearby fuel (or each other); (2) by percussion, in which a spark ignites fuel; (3) by using a lens to focus light—which is a way to concentrate its heat—on fuel.

✧✧✧It's a Fact!✧✧✧

People mostly used the percussion method (using flint and steel) up until 1827, when matches were invented. Matches use friction to ignite combustible chemicals on the match head.

It is thought that early humans first encountered fire that occurred naturally, such as seeing a tree that had been set on fire by a lightning bolt. Then they learned how to take fire from these sources and use it. After that, they learned to make it for themselves by rubbing sticks together to create friction or by striking certain rocks (usually flint) together to create sparks. Finally, they learned how to control fire, such as how to use it to make metals. They are us. This is why you were able to be a master of fire before you knew any of this (and why you are smart enough to be careful with it).

Questions to Ponder

1. What are the three ways by which people can make fire?

2. What is fuel?

3. Which material is usually part of the percussion method?

4. Everything is made of atoms. What does a fire tell you about the atoms of whatever is burning?

5. If you were stranded on a deserted island without matches or a lighter, would you try to make fire? How would you try? If you succeeded, what would you use it for?

The Northern (and Southern) Lights

Sometimes at latitudes near Earth's North and South Poles, nature puts on a display of lights of various colors that dance and swirl in the sky. These are the *aurora polaris*, or polar lights. The ones near the North Pole are called *aurora borealis* (northern lights), and the ones near the South Pole are called *aurora australis* (southern lights).

Charged particles are always flowing from the sun, and this flow is called the "solar wind." (This is the condition that makes comets seem as if they have tails.) Some of the solar wind gets caught up in Earth's magnetic field. Because of the way this field is on Earth, the particles that make up the solar wind are pulled near the poles. As they collide with gas particles in the atmosphere, the collision excites the gas particles (causes them to move faster). This excitement is what gives off light—and when there is enough excitement, we see the polar lights.

> ### ✦✦✦It's a Fact!✦✦✦
> The solar wind travels from the sun towards Earth at about 300 miles per second. Once it gets here, it produces the polar lights at 50–600 miles above Earth's surface.

Generally, both the northern and southern lights can be seen only within 30 degrees latitude of the poles—in other words, in the arctic and the Antarctic. However, the northern lights have been seen at times as far south as Florida, and the southern lights as far north as New Zealand. The intensity of the polar lights seems to go through an 11-year cycle, a cycle that seems to be exactly the opposite of the sunspot cycle on the sun . . . but no one is sure why this is.

Questions to Ponder

1. Where are you most likely to see the northern and southern lights?

2. Name two observable effects of the solar wind.

3. What does "aurora" mean?

4. How does the solar wind cause the northern and southern lights?

5. What do you think people thought about the northern and southern lights before they had any idea of what they really were?

The Cheetah and the Snail

THE WORLD ALMANAC

You've probably heard the tale of the tortoise and the hare. In this famous fable, a slow but clever tortoise challenges a quick but not-so-clever hare to a race. The hare is much faster—there is no way it can lose! But it gets too confident and takes a nap, sure that it can make up the time with its pure speed advantage. You know how it ends: the hare sleeps too long, and the tortoise wins the race.

Of course, this is just a fable. There are several valuable messages conveyed in it: "slow and steady wins the race," don't underestimate your opponent, and carelessness can cancel out ability.

✧✧✧It's a Fact!✧✧✧

The fable "The Tortoise and the Hare" is credited to Aesop, a legendary Greek fabulist who lived in the 6th century B.C. Aesop's fables were translated and handed down by many other Greek writers.

But what would really happen if a tortoise raced a hare? Could the underdog tortoise use sheer cleverness to outfox the hare? It's highly unlikely. A hare is over 200 times as fast as a tortoise! Hares (which are very similar to rabbits) can travel up to 35 mph (56 kph), whereas tortoises can only reach maximum speeds of .17 mph (.27 kph). You would have a better chance of outrunning a cheetah, the world's fastest animal, than that tortoise would have of winning the race.

Maximum Speeds of Selected Animals

Animal	mph	Animal	mph	Animal	mph
Cheetah	70	Hyena	40	Elephant	25
Antelope	61	Zebra	40	Black mamba snake	20
Wildebeest	50	Greyhound	39.4	Wild turkey	15
Lion	50	Whippet	35.5	Squirrel	12
Gazelle	50	Rabbit (domestic)	35	Pig (domestic)	11
Quarterhorse	47.5	Reindeer	32	Chicken	9
Elk	45	Giraffe	32	Spider	1.17
Cape hunting dog	45	Grizzly bear	30	Giant tortoise	0.17
Coyote	43	Cat (domestic)	30	Three-toed sloth	0.15
Gray fox	42	Human	27.9	Garden snail	0.03

═══ Questions to Ponder ═══

1. Hares are very similar to what kind of animal?

2. A domestic cat is how many times as fast as a squirrel?

3. What is the fastest reptile on this list?

4. Which item best answers this question: About how long ago did Aesop live?

    a. 1,400 years   b. 2,500 years   c. 3,600 years

5. Have you ever underestimated someone and then been taught a lesson by that person? Explain.

World Geography and Travel

What's Inside . . . .

Be a World Traveler

Have you ever heard the phrase, "There's a whole world outside your door"? As recently as a century ago, world travel was possible for only the wealthiest among us. Now, one can jet from country to country in relative safety and comfort. And while airfare is certainly not free, it is a luxury available to all and affordable to many.

So where will you go? To what places might you venture in the years to come? Here are a few sights to behold in each of the following cities:

Beijing (China)

✈ walk along the ancient Great Wall of China, one of the world's most famous tourist attractions

✈ visit the Forbidden City in the center of Beijing; there you will find the Palace Museum

Cairo (Egypt)

✈ explore the pyramids of Giza and the Sphinx, a structure in stone of a creature that is half man, half lion

✈ walk the halls of Al Azhar University, the oldest university in the world

Paris (France)

✈ view the famous Mona Lisa at the Louvre Museum

✈ view the entire city from the topmost level of the Eiffel Tower

San Francisco (California, U.S.A.)

✈ climb Coit Tower and take in the breathtaking views of the San Francisco Bay, Golden Gate Bridge, and Alcatraz Island

✈ take a cable car to the top of Lombard Street and walk down North America's most crooked street

Air Distance (in Miles) Between Selected World Cities

	Beijing	Cairo	London	Los Angeles	New York	Paris	San Francisco	Tokyo
Beijing	...	4,698	5,074	6,250	6,844	5,120	5,918	1,307
Cairo	4,698	...	2,185	7,520	5,619	1,998	7,466	5,958
London	5,074	2,185	...	5,439	3,469	214	5,367	5,959
Los Angeles	6,250	7,520	5,439	...	2,451	5,601	347	5,470
New York	6,844	5,619	3,469	2,451	...	3,636	2,572	6,757
Paris	5,120	1,998	214	5,601	3,636	...	5,577	6,053
San Francisco	5,918	7,466	5,367	347	2,572	5,577	...	5,150
Tokyo	1,307	5,958	5,959	5,470	6,757	6,053	5,150	...

Questions to Ponder

1. How many miles is it by air from Los Angeles to Beijing?

2. How many more miles is it by air from London to Tokyo than it is from Cairo to Tokyo?

3. If you were visiting the Eiffel Tower and wanted to travel to see the oldest university in the world, how many miles would you have to travel by air?

4. Which of the cities listed above is on the continent of Africa?

5. If you could travel to one city outside of your country, where would you go and why?

From Country to Country

If you have a passport, you know that it's a little booklet that you get stamped when you go from country to country. You also know that it's got your basic personal information: name, address, date of birth, etc. And, of course, you've seen that great little picture of you! What you might not have paid attention to is the thing that really makes it what it is: a short letter from your government asking that whatever countries you travel to let you enter and exit them safely.

The basic idea behind passports dates back at least as far as about 450 B.C., when Nehemiah, a servant of King Artaxerxes of Persia, asked to travel to Judah. The King granted his request, and he also gave Nehemiah a letter "to the governors of the province beyond the river" which requested that Nehemiah be allowed to travel safely throughout Judah.

The stamps that are put in passports are called *visas*. Visas are the official way in which a government gives the person holding the passport permission to enter and exit a country—basically, like Judah saying "yes" to King Artaxerxes' request. Some countries require you to get this permission before traveling to that country; otherwise, they may not let you in. This often depends on the relations between your

✦✦✦It's a Fact!✦✦✦

Some countries have agreements with certain others that make it so you don't need a passport to travel between them. This usually has to do with how close the countries are geographically—assuming, of course, that their governments like each other (which, sadly, is not always the case). The U.S. has such an agreement with both of its neighbors, Canada and Mexico.

government and the government of the country you wish to enter. For example, relations between the United States and England have been very close for a very long time; so, if you're an American traveling to England, you generally will have no trouble getting right into the country. But you wouldn't want to try without your passport, because a passport is also what tells other governments who you are . . . and they want to know.

Questions to Ponder

1. What is the idea behind passports?

2. When would you need a passport?

3. What is a visa?

4. For at least how long has the basic idea behind passports been around?

5. What is the first (or next) country you would like to go to where you would need your passport? Why that country?

Why They're There

We may climb mountains simply because they are there, but mountains don't exist because we climb them. The reason they exist is that Earth is constantly changing, for the land on which we live is constantly in motion.

The entire crust (or surface) of Earth—including the land beneath the oceans—is an assembly of sections of rock, called plates. The plates are in constant motion, and, although this motion appears almost non-existent to us in our day-to-day lives (the plates move only a few centimeters each year), it is the motion of the plates relative to each other that creates mountains. Think of it this way: we have six continents today (if you count Europe and Asia, which are connected, as one). But originally they were all one super-continent. It is the movements of these plates, called plate tectonics, that account for the difference today. Two (or more) of these plates grinding together triggers various geological processes which result in what is called *crustal uplift*. Basically, this means that, as the plates are pressed together, the action folds the land upwards. If these folds aren't big, we call them hills; but if they are big enough, we call them mountains. Often a fold is not only big but also very long. When that happens, the fold may be higher in some places than in others—and we call these mountain ranges! Another way mountains form is by *volcanism*—and, as you would expect from the way the term sounds, mountains formed this way are volcanoes. Volcanoes form when molten rock (rock so hot that it's liquid) accumulates in one spot beneath Earth's surface. Eventually, it can force the land above it upwards, which can result in any one of five types of volcanoes (although only three are what we tend to think of as mountains). The size and shape of a mountain are affected not only by plate tectonics. For example, in the case of a volcano, the size can increase by the build-up of cooled lava, or it can decrease by an eruption that blows part of it away. But it is erosion that affects all mountains, since things like wind and rain are always wearing them away.

> ### ⋄⋄⋄**It's a Fact!**⋄⋄⋄
>
> In a matter of moments, the height of Mt. Saint Helens in Washington was reduced from 9,677 feet to 8,365 feet when it erupted on March 27, 1980.

World's Tallest Mountains (ranked by elevation above sea level)

Name	Place	Height (ft.)	Name	Place	Height (ft.)
1. Everest	Nepal-Tibet	29,035	6. Lhotse II	Nepal-Tibet	27,560
2. K2	Kashmir	28,250	7. Dhaulagiri	Nepal	26,810
3. Kanchenjunga	India-Nepal	28,208	8. Manaslu I	Nepal	26,760
4. Lhotse I	Nepal-Tibet	27,923	9. Cho Oyu	Nepal-Tibet	26,750
5. Makalu I	Nepal-Tibet	27,824	10. Nanga Parbat	Kashmir	26,660

Questions to Ponder

1. What are the names of the two ways in which mountains form?

2. How much shorter is Mt. Saint Helens today than the sixth-tallest mountain in the world?

3. What does "geological" mean?

4. Most of the world's highest mountains are located in Nepal and/or Tibet. What is the most likely reason for this?

5. Do you think the same things that make and change mountains affect the rest of the earth? Explain your answer.

Country or Continent?

Australia is a *country*. Australia is a *continent*. How can it be both? The answer is simple: *countries* are made by humans, *continents* by nature. Australia is the world's smallest continent, but also its sixth-largest country.

Like all continents, Australia was once part of Pangaea, the "supercontinent." A section called Gondwanaland broke off and drifted east. About 200 million years ago Antarctica broke off from this and began drifting south, leaving Australia by itself. Exploration of Australia by westerners did not really begin until the 17th century, even though it had been guessed that there was a large land mass just about where Australia really is. The Netherlands was the first country to really explore the continent and its surrounding waters, but they were not interested in settling (establishing permanent places for people to live) the continent. Instead, it was Great Britain that came to colonize Australia. This truly began after that nation had lost America's War of Independence. You see, prior to that defeat, Britain had shipped many of its convicts (people found guilty of committing a crime) to its American colony. With that gone—and with Britain experiencing an increase in its number of convicts and a shortage of where to put them—it decided that Australia was just the place. In 1787, Britain's first prison settlement was established on Australia with over 400 seamen and 750 convicts. The English government official responsible for this first permanent settlement on Australia was Lord Sydney—and it is after him that what would become Australia's largest city was named.

Over time, British military personnel also came to be stationed on Australia, free British citizens came to settle there, and convicts completed their sentences and remained on the continent, sometimes being given land and employment. Eventually, certain sections of Australia were founded as British colonies. Later, these colonies united, and on Jan. 1, 1901, the Commonwealth of Australia was officially recognized as independent by Great Britain. Australia the continent had also become Australia the country.

> ◇◇◇**It's a Fact!**◇◇◇
>
> The first people on Australia were the Aborigines, who lived there at least as far back as 40,000 years ago. When the British began to colonize Australia in the 18th century, a great many Aborigines died from British diseases (for which their bodies had no immunities) and mistreatment. Although remaining Aborigines eventually became part of the Australian population, as recently as 1971 they were still being treated so badly that they weren't even included in that country's census. Today, Australia's original people make up only about 1.5% of the total population.

Questions to Ponder

1. When was Australia first officially recognized as a country?

2. All continents were once part of a single land mass, which eventually broke into pieces. To which current continent was Australia most recently attached?

3. About how many people were part of Australia's first permanent settlement?

4. Which country was the first to thoroughly explore Australia?

5. Many Australians feel that some of the land taken from the Aborigines should be given back to them. Do you think this is a good or bad idea? Explain.

World's Tallest Buildings

The two tallest buildings in the world are the Petronas Towers in Kuala Lumpur, Malaysia. Each 88-story tower is 1,483 feet tall. A double-decker skybridge, measuring 192 feet in length, joins the two towers at the 41st and 42nd floors.

The towers—which house the headquarters for many corporations and companies, as well as an 864-seat concert hall—were officially opened on August 31, 1999, in an event that signified Malaysia's growth as an up-and-coming industrialized nation.

> ❖❖❖**It's a Fact**❖❖❖
>
> The Petronas Towers were designed by Cesar Pelli, the architect who also designed the World Financial Center in New York City. The buildings of the World Financial Center were designed to blend in with the neighboring—and much-larger—twin towers of the World Trade Center, which collapsed as a result of terrorist attacks on September 11, 2001.

30 Tallest Buildings in the World

Name, Year, City, Country	Height	Stories	Name, Year, City, Country	Height	Stories
Petronas Tower I, 1998, Kuala Lumpu Malaysia	1,483	88	Baiyoke Tower II, 1998, Bangkok, Thailand	1,050	90
Petronas Tower II, 1998, Kuala Lumpur, Malaysia	1,483	88	Chrysler Bldg., 1930, New York, U.S.	1,046	77
Sears Tower, 1974, Chicago, IL, U.S.	1,450	110	Bank of America Plaza, 1993, Atlanta, GA, U.S.	1,023	55
Jin Mao Bldg., 1998, Shanghai, China	1,381	88	Library Tower, 1990, Los Angeles, CA, U.S.	1,018	73
CITIC Plaza, 1997, Guangzhou, China	1,283	80	Telekom Malaysia Headquarters, 1999, Kuala Lumpur, Malaysia	1,017	55
Shun Hing Square, 1996, Shenzhen, China	1,260	69	Emirates Towers Two, 2000, Dubai, U.A.E.	1,014	54
Empire State Building, 1931, New York, U.S.	1,250	102	AT&T Corporate Center, 1989, Chicago, IL, U.S.	1,007	60
Central Plaza, 1992, Hong Kong, China	1,227	78	Chase Tower, 1982, Houston, TX, U.S.	1,000	75
Bank of China, 1989, Hong Kong, China	1,209	70	Two Prudential Plaza, 1990, Chicago, IL, U.S.	995	64
Emirates Towers One, 2000, Dubai, U.A.E.	1,165	55	Ryugyong Hotel, 1995, Pyongyang, North Korea	984	105
The Centre, 1998, Hong Kong, China	1,148	79	Commerzbank Tower, 1997, Frankfurt, Germany	981	63
Tuntex & Chein-Tai Tower, 1998, Kaohsiung, Taiwan	1,140	85	Wells Fargo Plaza, 1983, Houston, TX, U.S.	972	71
Aon Center, 1973, Chicago, IL, U.S.	1,136	80	Landmark Tower, 1993, Yokohama, Japan	971	70
Kingdom Centre, 2001, Riyadh, Saudi Arabia	1,132	30	311 S. Wacker Drive, Chicago, IL, U.S.	961	65
John Hancock Center, 1969, Chicago, IL, U.S.	1,127	100			
Burj al Arab Hotel, 1999, Dubai, U.A.E	1,053	60			

Questions to Ponder

1. Before the Petronas Towers were built, which building was the tallest in the world and in which city and country is it located?

2. Which is the tallest building in Europe? How tall is it, and in what city and country is it located?

3. If you were reading an almanac from 1950, which building would it list as the tallest in the world? When was this structure built, and where is it located?

4. What is the average height per story of the Petronas Towers?

5. After the events of September 11, 2001, in which both towers of the World Trade Center in New York collapsed due to terrorist attacks, how would you feel about visiting the top floors of any of the world's tallest buildings?

Water Falls

Gravity affects water in the same way it affects everything else. Sometimes one part of a river or stream becomes significantly lower than a nearby part, and the difference in height affects the way in which the water flows. In other words, water falls.

Waterfalls form in several ways. The main way is erosion. In some streams, different parts of the streambed are made up of different types of rock, some of which get worn away by water more rapidly than others. A waterfall can form eventually where stronger and weaker rock meet. As the weaker rock wears away more rapidly, that part of the streambed sinks, changing the course of the water. This change becomes more and more rapid, since the water flowing from the stronger portion of the streambed hits the weaker part with increasing strength because it is coming from increasingly higher up. Sometimes the weaker portions break off in chunks. This is how some of the largest waterfalls in the world, such as Niagara Falls in North

> ❖❖❖**It's a Fact!**❖❖❖
>
> The height of a waterfall refers to how far its water drops. Height has nothing to do with how much water flows over the falls, which is called the volume. For example, Niagara Falls has the greatest volume of any waterfall in the world—more than twice as much as any other waterfall—and yet its drop is less than 200 feet.

America and Victoria Falls in Africa, were formed. A similar type of waterfall results when a fault (a break or rift in the earth) raises a mountain range or part of a range, creating what is called a fault scarp, over which streams drop steeply. In the mountains, waterfalls can form where a glacier has deepened one part of a valley and changes the land the water is flowing over. This type of waterfall is called a cascade. The main difference between cascades and other waterfalls is that the water in cascades never leaves its bed, while other waterfalls feature free-falling water. Many cascades fall a great distance and are actually a series of falls.

World's Highest Waterfalls

Name	Location	Height (ft.)	Name	Location	Height (ft.)
Angel	Venezuela	3,312	Yosemite	U.S.	2,425
Tungela	South Africa	2,800	Espelands	Norway	2,307
Utigord	Norway	2,625	Lower Mar Valley	Norway	2,151
Monge	Norway	2,540	Tyssestrengene	Norway	2,123
Mutarazi	Zimbabwe	2,499	Cuquenan	Venezuela	2,000

═══ Questions to Ponder ═══

1. What is the main process by which waterfalls form?

2. What is the name for the type of waterfall which does not feature free-falling water?

3. How many waterfalls in the world are over half a mile in height?

4. Cuquenan Falls is in Venezuela and, at 2,000 feet in height, is the 10th-highest waterfall in the world. From this information, what can you determine about its volume? Explain how you can determine this.

5. From time to time some waterfalls stop flowing, either temporarily or permanently. This can be for either natural or man-made reasons. This has happened even to Niagara Falls! Describe a waterfall (real or imaginary). Now, imagine it has stopped flowing. Describe what stopped it, and what it looks like without any water.

The Undersea Train

England and France are not very far apart—as close as 34 km in one place. But they are separated by a body of water, the English Channel. People have been able to boat between the two countries for a thousand years, and for a hundred years people have been able to fly between them. However, boating isn't the quickest way to travel such a distance, but it's very short to bother with flying. What would be the best way to make such a trip if you couldn't drive it? By train! This thinking is what led to one of the greatest feats of engineering in the 20th century: the Channel Tunnel, or *Chunnel*.

✧✧✧**It's a Fact!**✧✧✧

The Chunnel is never actually in the English Channel itself. Instead, it runs 150 meters beneath the sea bed. In all, 7 million tons of rubble was removed to make the Chunnel—more than enough to build three of the world's biggest pyramids. This rubble was deposited in England, increasing the size of the country by the size of 68 football fields. This area has been made into a park.

The idea for the Chunnel goes all the way back to 1802, when French mining engineer Albert Mathieu-Favier suggested it. Of course, a proposal to build a long tunnel under the sea is easier suggested than done! Different people tried to figure out how to do it over most of the coming century. In 1875, the Channel Tunnel Company was formed with the permission of both the English and French governments. Another company was also given the rights to try in 1881. Tunneling was started several times over the next 70 years, but was always stopped for various reasons. In 1960, the Channel Tunnel Study Group gained approval for its plan, and some work was done over the next 15 years—but *again* construction was stopped. Finally, in 1987 a company called Eurotunnel took over, and, using the Channel Tunnel Study Group's scheme, tunneling companies from each direction met in the middle in December of 1990. Four years later, the Chunnel was in full service. At the height of construction, 15,000 people were working on the Chunnel.

The Chunnel is actually comprised of three tunnels: one track for each direction and a service tunnel (for maintenance and to evacuate passengers on foot in case of an emergency) that runs in between them. The Chunnel runs underneath the Channel for 39 kilometers. Up to 600 trains can run in any one day. The trains run at about 130 km/hour (80 mph), and each is about a half-mile long. Some of them are "drive-on/drive-off" trains, in which people in cars drive right on a train in one country, ride through the Chunnel, then drive off in the other. Trains can carry as many as 180 cars.

Questions to Ponder

1. Where is the Chunnel?

2. How long was it between the time that someone first thought of the idea for the Chunnel and when the project was fully completed?

3. What is the name of the company that was in charge of the building project at the time it was completed?

4. How long does it take a train to go underneath the English Channel?

5. What do you think might be two benefits of two countries working together on a project like the Chunnel? What might be two potential problems?

Frontier Forests

About 8,000 years ago humans became advanced enough to disturb the world's natural environment on a large scale. At that time, it is estimated that there were about 62 million acres of forest on the planet. Since then, almost half of that forest has been completely destroyed. Also, more than half of the forest remaining is not in its original condition—that is, it exists as only small fragments of the forest it was originally part of or it has been planted by man. The forest that's left in original condition is called frontier forest.

Frontier forests are ecosystems, which means they are like single, giant, living organisms, with all parts (plants, animals, trees, rivers, insects, etc.) interacting with and supporting each other. One of the best examples of a frontier forest is in the Amazon River basin in Brazil. About 65% of all the varieties of plant life in Brazil can be found only in this rain forest. But what happens here affects not just Brazil but the entire planet. For example, it is estimated that at least 15% of the world's oxygen comes from this rain forest alone, and that about 20% of the world's fresh-water cycle flows through its river system.

Even though about four-fifths of the world's frontier forests have been destroyed by humans, much of what is left is still being threatened by such practices as logging and mining. Many people are alarmed by this, and in recent years there has been an increased awareness of the need to protect what we have left.

Frontier Forest Area (selected countries)

Country	% of Orig. Remaining	% of World Total	% Threatened
Russia	29	26	19
Canada	58	25	21
Brazil	42	17	48
Peru	57	4	95
Indonesia	28	4	54
Venezuela	59	3	37
Colombia	36	3	19
United States	6	2	85
Zaire	16	2	70
Bolivia	44	2	97
Papua/New Guinea	40	1	84
Chile	55	1	76

Questions to Ponder

1. What are frontier forests?
2. How much of the original forest on Earth has been destroyed? About what percentage of frontier forests remain?
3. How are the countries ordered in the table above?
4. Which of the listed countries still have more than half of their original forest with less than half of it being threatened?
5. Do you think it's possible for a country to progress while leaving its frontier forests untouched? Why or why not?

The Bottom of the World

There is one continent in the world on which no country stakes a claim, and that is Antarctica. Instead, the nations of the world have decided to set aside this icy land for scientific research. There is no government, no leadership; and scientists from all over the world share the entire continent.

❖❖❖It's a Fact!❖❖❖

Antarctica is the coldest continent on Earth, both because of its location on the planet and its being the world's highest continent (with an average elevation of over 6,500 feet). The coldest temperature ever recorded was at Russia's Vostok Station:
-129 degrees F
on July 21, 1983.

It was not until the 1770s that it was known that there was any land this far south on the planet, and it was 1821 before it was realized that Antarctica (which means *opposite of the arctic*) was a continent. No people lived there, and only 2.4% of Antarctica's area (which is bigger than Australia) is exposed rock, the rest being covered by ice—so much ice that the rest of the world combined contains only ⅛ as much. Largely because of this, by 1920 only about 5% of the continent had been explored, but owing to advances in aviation over the next 20 years most of the coast and several of Antarctica's inland areas had been at least photographed. During this period many countries began to claim different parts of Antarctica, but beginning in the late 1950s, 12 countries agreed to work together to conduct scientific research of the continent. In 1959 these 12 countries signed the Antarctic Treaty, which states that Antarctica be used only for peaceful purposes, that no sort of military activity may take place, and that everyone is free to conduct scientific investigations there. Added to that treaty in 1991 were provisions that no drilling for oil or mining for minerals may be done. Currently, about 20 nations have scientific bases in Antarctica—but the continent still has no permanent residents, as scientists usually stay between one and two years.

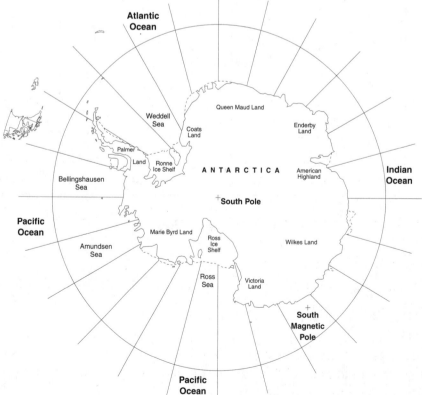

The Bottom of the World *(cont.)*

Antarctic Exploration and Developments

— 1773–1820 . . . . Beginning with James Cook (G.B.), many explorers approach Antarctica, sighting outer islands.

— 1820 . . . . Nathaniel Palmer (U.S.) reaches a peninsula of the continent itself . . . without realizing that this is a continent.

— Feb. 7, 1821 . . . . John Davis (U.S.) makes first known landing on Antarctica . . . although he doesn't know he's on a continent.

— 1823 . . . . James Weddell (G.B.) discovers what came to be known as Weddell Sea, the southernmost point that had yet been reached.

— 1840 . . . . Charles Wilkes (U.S.) follows the coast for 1,500 miles and is the first to realize that this is a continent.

— 1841–'42 . . . . Ross Ice Shelf found by James Clark Ross (G.B.).

— 1895 . . . . Leonard Kristensen (Nor.) is first to go ashore on main continental mass.

— 1899 . . . . C. E. Borchgrevink (Nor.), a member of Kristensen's 1895 party, returns with a British party, and they are the first to spend a winter there.

— 1902–'04 . . . . Robert Falcon Scott (G.B.) expedition

— 1908–'08 . . . . Ernest Shackleton (G.B.) expedition; discovers route that would lead to South Pole.

— Dec. 14, 1911 . . . . . . Roald Amundsen (Nor.) leads four men (on dog sleds) to South Pole.

— 1928 . . . . George Hubert Wilkins (Aus.) is the first person to use a plane over Antarctica.

— 1929 . . . . Richard E. Byrd (U.S.) establishes Little America on Bay of Whales.

— 1939–'41 . . . . U.S. Navy planes discover 150,000 sq. mi. of land.

— 1940 . . . . Byrd charts large chunk of coast.

— 1946–'47 . . . . U.S. Navy photomaps entire coastline.

— July 1957–Dec. '58 . . International Geophysical Year: 12 nations cooperate for scientific research.

— 1958 . . . . U.S. scientists see from ground what had earlier been seen from the air: Dufek Massif, a huge mountain range.

— 1959 . . . . Antarctic Treaty signed by Argentina, Australia, Belgium, Britain, Chile, France, Japan, New Zealand, Norway, South Africa, the U.S., and the U.S.S.R.

— 1962 . . . . First nuclear power plant begins operation.

— 1985 . . . . Igor A. Zotikov (U.S.S.R.) finds evidence supporting continental drift theory.

— 1991 . . . . 24 nations extend Antarctic Treaty, adding that drilling and mining are prohibited in Antarctica.

Questions to Ponder

1. Antarctica is part of which countries?

2. In the name "Antarctica," what does the prefix "ant" (a variation of "anti") mean?

3. What percentage of the world's ice is in Antarctica?

4. What tool made exploration of Antarctica easier after 1920?

5. It is almost certain that there are many natural resources in Antarctica, such as oil and many minerals. Do you think it is a good or bad idea to have added to the Antarctic Treaty prohibitions against drilling and mining? Explain your reasoning.

From Fiction to Fact

In 1873, Jules Verne published what would become his most famous novel, *Around the World in 80 Days*. In that book, the main character makes a bet that he can circumnavigate the globe (travel around the world) in 80 days—something thought to be impossible. In the fictional world he succeeds, but many people of the time believed that such a thing could not happen in the real world. In 1889, however, someone decided to find out.

◆◆◆It's a Fact!◆◆◆

The Jules Verne Trophy is awarded to whoever goes around the world the fastest . . . in a boat. It is currently held by Bruno Peyron and his crew, who completed the circumnavigation in May of 2002 in 64 days, 8 hours, and 37 minutes.

A newspaper called *The New York World* decided to send one of its reporters, Nellie Bly, on an around-the-world trip to see if Verne's fiction could be turned into a reality. Remember, this was before the invention of the airplane—and even before cars were very advanced—so the trip had to be made mostly by ship and by train—although some of the travel on land had to be done in other ways, including horse and burro. But on January 25, 1890, Bly arrived in New York, from where she had departed a little over 72 days and 6 hours earlier.

As time went by and technology advanced, people were able to go around the world in shorter and shorter times. Trains got faster and more tracks were laid, cars improved and more roads were built. But the most important invention for around-the-world travel was the airplane. Although not invented until 1903, by 1931 the around-the-world record had been set by airplane—and that record was a lot faster than anything that had come before: 8 days, 15 hours, and 51 minutes! By 1949 that record had been cut to a mere 94 hours and 1 minute. Today, however, we live in a different era, for it takes a space shuttle only about 90 minutes to circle the globe.

Questions to Ponder

1. Who wrote *Around the World in 80 Days*?

2. How many years after the main character of *Around the World in 80 Days* circumnavigated the globe did someone do it in real life?

3. What company did Nellie Bly work for when she first went around the world?

4. How many times could a space shuttle circle the world in 80 days?

5. If you had a chance to travel around the world, how would you want to do it? Explain (and be as creative as you like).

Jules Verne

The Arts

Award-Winning Books

Think about all of those novels your teacher has assigned you to read. Some of them—like *Out of the Dust* or *A Single Shard*—give you a glimpse of what it was like to live in a different time or place in history, such as the Great Depression or 12th-century Korea. Others—like *A Wrinkle in Time* or any *Harry Potter* book—share with you worlds that no one has ever seen or even imagined before. Hopefully, some of these books you have read in school instantly became your favorites. Others? Let's just say that you may be in no hurry to read some of them again.

◆◆◆It's a Fact!◆◆◆

Established in 1922, the Newbery Medal is named for John Newbery, an 18th-century British bookseller. He devoted much of his life to writing and publishing books that were aimed to both entertain and instruct children. By publishing these books, he established juvenile literature as an important branch of the publishing business.

A book that appeals to you might not appeal to the person sitting next to you. When a particular book (or movie, song, TV show, etc.) appeals to a lot of people, it is successful. But does that necessarily make it "the best" book or "the best" T.V. show? In what ways can you judge whether or not one piece of art is better than another?

Each year, the Association for Library Service to Children (a division of the American Library Association) reviews all of the books published by American authors in that year and tries to decide which one is the best. This Association is made up of public and school librarians. They make every effort to judge the books on their literary quality for children, and not on a book's popularity or the political nature of its message. In the end, the winning book is awarded an honor called the Newbery Medal for "making the biggest contribution to American literature for children."

Newbery Medal Winners (1990–2002)

Year	Book	Author	Year	Book	Author
1990	*Number the Stars*	Lois Lowry	1996	*The Midwife's Apprentice*	Karen Cushman
1991	*Maniac Magee*	Jerry Spinelli	1997	*The View from Saturday*	E.L. Konigsburg
1992	*Shiloh*	Phyllis Reynolds Naylor	1998	*Out of the Dust*	Karen Hesse
			1999	*Holes*	Louis Sachar
1993	*Missing May*	Cynthia Rylant	2000	*Bud, Not Buddy*	Christopher Paul Curtis
1994	*The Giver*	Lois Lowry	2001	*A Year Down Under*	Richard Peck
1995	*Walk Two Moons*	Sharon Creech	2002	*A Single Shard*	Linda Sue Park

Questions to Ponder

1. Which author wrote two books that received Newbery Medals in the 1990s?

2. What does the word "juvenile" mean?

3. Who was John Newbery?

4. Are any of the books on the Newbery Medal list among your favorites? Are there any books written since 1990 that you think should have won a Newbery Medal but didn't?

5. Do you think it's fair to judge a book, CD, or movie by how many people buy it or pay to see it? Does popularity equal artistic success?

The King of Museums

There are many museums, many great museums. However, there is one museum that is known throughout the entire world: the Louvre (pronounced "LOOV"). The Louvre is France's national museum. It is located in Paris, on the right bank of the Seine River, and it houses one of the world's greatest art collections.

The Louvre began to be built in 1546, but not as a museum. It was originally a palace—and not just any palace, but one in which the kings of France lived up until 1682. The original structure was added to all the way up until the middle of the 19th century, and today it is still one of the world's biggest palaces. It was opened to the public as a museum in 1793, and it contains many types of art, including sculpture (such as the *Venus de Milo*) and jewelry. The Louvre also contains many antiquities (very old items) from ancient cultures such as the Greek, Roman, and

> ❖❖❖**It's a Fact!**❖❖❖
>
> France was invaded in both World War I and World War II. During these years, all of the Louvre's masterpieces were moved to secret hiding places so that they would not be stolen or damaged.

Egyptian empires. Many of these were taken by the French when they conquered foreign countries. Napoleon, for example, brought back from his campaigns (fighting) in Egypt so many antiquities that a new section of the Louvre was opened just to display these. But it is the Louvre's paintings that make it so famous. There are more than 6,000, many by history's most famous artists, such as Rembrandt, Leonardo da Vinci (including his *Mona Lisa*), El Greco, Raphael, and Goya.

The Louvre was recently involved in a controversy—not about the art inside, but about some outside. A renovation (fixing, making like new again) of the museum was completed in 1993. Part of this was a glass pyramid that was built as an entrance. The pyramid was built in a completely different style than the Louvre itself, and many people hated it because of this . . . but others thought it was a great and interesting addition. One thing's for sure: it gets your attention!

Questions to Ponder

1. Where is the Louvre?

2. How long was it between when the king stopped living in the Louvre and it was opened as a museum?

3. Who painted *Mona Lisa*?

4. What does the verb "to house" mean?

5. France has now given back many works of art that it took from other countries in earlier times, even though some of them had been in France for a very long time. Do you think it was good for France to give these back; or do you think that, since they had been in the Louvre for so long and since anyone who wanted could go see them there, that France should have left them in the museum? Explain your answer.

The Boss

Film is an art form comprised of many parts. An average film includes photography, writing, acting, lighting, costuming, music—and that's just to name a few! But in the making of a film, there is only one person who is really the boss: the director.

Once a script is chosen and actors are cast, it is the director who makes almost every decision about what goes into a film. On location, this includes how the camera moves, how actors move and say their lines, if any lines need to be changed, how a shot looks, and when a scene has been done well enough to move on to a different one. Even when the filming is complete, the director's work is not. There is still much to do, including deciding what sound or music will make a scene play out just right onscreen, which shots will end up in the final version of the film, and how those shots will be edited together.

Many who enjoy film do not understand how much work directors do, but those who understand film well are fully aware of it. Among the Academy Awards, for example, a Best Director award is given each year. Also, many experts in the history of film consider directors much more important to the overall film than actors—even though the actors are generally much more famous.

Directors Who Have Won Multiple Academy Awards (for Best Director)

Director	Films Won For (Year)
John Ford	*The Informer* (1935), *The Grapes of Wrath* (1940), *How Green Was My Valley* (1941), *The Quiet Man* (1952)
William Wyler	*Mrs. Miniver* (1942), *The Best Years of Our Lives* (1946), *Ben Hur* (1959)
Frank Capra	*It Happened One Night* (1934), *Mr. Deeds Goes to Town* (1936), *You Can't Take It With You* (1938)
Frank Borzage	*Seventh Heaven* (1928), *Bad Girl* (1932)
Frank Lloyd	*The Divine Lady* (1929), *Cavalcade* (1933)
Leo McCarey	*The Awful Truth* (1937), *Going My Way* (1944)
Billy Wilder	*The Lost Weekend* (1945), *The Apartment* (1960)
Elia Kazan	*Gentleman's Agreement* (1947), *On the Waterfront* (1954)
Joseph L. Mankiewicz	*A Letter to Three Wives* (1949), *All About Eve* (1950)
George Stevens	*A Place in the Sun* (1951), *Giant* (1956)
Fred Zinnemann	*From Here to Eternity* (1953), *A Man for All Seasons* (1966)
David Lean	*A Bridge on the River Kwai* (1957), *Lawrence of Arabia* (1962)
Milos Forman	*One Flew Over the Cuckoo's Nest* (1975), *Amadeus* (1984)
Oliver Stone	*Platoon* (1986), *Born on the Fourth of July* (1989)
Steven Spielberg	*Schindler's List* (1993), *Saving Private Ryan* (1998)

Questions to Ponder

1. Have any directors won two Best Director awards in a row? If so, who?

2. Who was the first director to win a second Best Director award? When did he achieve this?

3. From the awards listed above, in which decade(s) were the most given? How many?

4. What does "comprised" mean?

5. John Ford has won four Best Director awards, more than anyone else. On the other hand, some film historians consider other directors to be worthy who have never won the award. How meaningful do you think winning awards is? Explain your answer.

Not Exactly a Failure

Unfortunately, being a great artist is no guarantee of being a great success. While a very few artists enjoy fame and fortune during their lives, most of them remain completely unknown for all time. Somewhere in between these two possibilities is what happened to Vincent van Gogh.

Van Gogh (correctly pronounced "van GAUGH" and *not* "van GO") was born in the Netherlands in 1853. By age 27 he had worked as a salesman, a tutor, a bookkeeper, and preacher for miners, but he was successful as none of these. For most of his life he was supported financially by his brother Theo. It was around 1880 that Vincent decided to become an artist. He studied drawing and painting, and soon he was painting constantly. However, even though Theo worked in an art gallery, Vincent's work did not find an audience during his lifetime. He died in 1890 having sold only one painting (for about $100) and feeling that he was a failure. But van Gogh's success as an artist after his death has been very different than it was in life. Today, van Gogh's paintings sell for millions of dollars. In fact, the highest price ever paid for a painting was for van Gogh's *Portrait of Doctor Gachet*, which sold for an incredible $82.5 million! Of course, how good a piece of art is doesn't necessarily have anything to do with how much people will pay for it. Otherwise, van Gogh's life might have gone quite differently!

Top 10 Highest Prices Paid for Paintings

Painting	Painter	Price	Year Paid
Portrait of Doctor Gachet	van Gogh	$82.5 million	1990
Au Moulin de la Galette	Renoir	$78.1 million	1990
Portrait de l'artiste sans barbe	van Gogh	$71.5 million	1998
Femme aux Bras Croisés	Picasso	$65 million	2000
Rideau, Cruchon et Compotier	Cezanne	$60 million	1999
Les Noces de Pierrette	Picasso	$51.56 million	1989
Femme Assise Dans un Jardin	Picasso	$49.5 million	1999
Irises	van Gogh	$49 million	1987
Le Rêve	Picasso	$48 million	1997
Self Portrait: Yo Picasso	Picasso	$47.85 million	1989

Questions to Ponder

1. Where was van Gogh born?

2. What is the main way that van Gogh got money to live on?

3. How long after van Gogh's death did one of his paintings sell for $49 million?

4. What fraction of the price paid for *Portrait of Doctor Gachet* did van Gogh earn from sales of his work during his lifetime?

5. How do you think it's possible that van Gogh's work could be so loved now and yet have been more or less ignored while he was alive?

Van Gogh's self portrait

More Than a Pop Group

In 2001, Paul McCartney released one of about two dozen albums that sold over two million copies during the year. This wouldn't be so remarkable if it weren't for the fact that McCartney has been releasing million-selling albums for almost 40 years. He has had a great career as a solo artist, but it was his time spent as a member of the Beatles that makes him a legend.

◆◆◆It's a Fact!◆◆◆

The Beatles did many unique things. One of them was to record parts of a song live during the world's first worldwide television program. The song, "All You Need Is Love", was a number-one hit not only in England and the U.S., but also in countries such as Argentina, Australia, Canada, Denmark, Ireland, Israel, New Zealand, Poland, Spain, Switzerland, and West Germany.

Although the Beatles existed as a group for less than a decade, they have sold more records than any group in history. "Beatlemania" was a term coined in the 1960s to describe the frenzy that they caused among their fans, for they were the first group of the "British Invasion," groups such as the Rolling Stones and the Who that came out of England and conquered the American music scene. There was no group like the Beatles, though. At one point they were so popular that during one week they had not only the number-one single on the pop charts, but they also had numbers two, three, four, and five. No other musical artist has come even close to doing this.

The Beatles—which were made up of McCartney, John Lennon, George Harrison, and Ringo Starr—were not only popular, they were revolutionary. Together with George Martin, their producer (the person who helps put the sounds of a recording together), they created new ways in which to record music, including releasing the first album that was recorded in stereo. The Beatles were probably the most loved group in history, and millions of people were upset when they broke up in 1970. However, the individual members continued to release music on their own, with McCartney and Lennon becoming major solo stars. They also used their fame on behalf of many causes. Lennon was particularly active in trying to promote peace. When he was murdered by an obsessed fan in 1980, the entire world mourned his passing. On record, though, he and the Beatles will be with us forever, and to this day they continue to sell many records. Several collections of Beatles songs have been released in the years since the band broke up, and they often debut on the charts at number one.

Questions to Ponder

1. What country did the Beatles come from?

2. Which of the Beatles had the biggest solo careers?

3. What is the highest percentage of the top-ten singles that were Beatles songs during a single week?

4. Name two "firsts" the Beatles were part of.

5. Think of another musical artist whose fame goes beyond the world of music, and then explain how that person or group has influenced society.

Challenging Freedom

In the United States—as in any country that considers itself free—no freedom is more important than the freedom of speech. It is not by chance that the First Amendment of the Bill of Rights guarantees this freedom. Freedom of speech includes the freedom to write and read whatever you choose. But some groups don't agree with this freedom. They feel that people shouldn't be allowed to say or write certain things. At times in history people have felt so strongly about this that they even burned books which they felt should not have been written. When books were not so easy to get this was an effective way to keep people from reading them. What happens more often now is that people try to have the books they don't like *banned*. But what does that mean?

To ban something is to forbid it. Sometimes a group of people in a certain area agree to challenge certain books, which means that they try to get them banned. They want these books banned for varied reasons. Often these reasons are religious, but not always: sometimes the reasons are political; sometimes people feel the books go against their personal moral beliefs; and sometimes people simply want to restrict certain books to an adult audience—something like the movie

> ✦✦✦**It's a Fact!**✦✦✦
>
> "Banned Books Week" occurs every fall, usually at the end of September. During this week, people are encouraged to read at least one book that has been banned at some time in history as a way of standing up for your freedom and rights.

rating system. The two places where people most often try to have books banned are in schools and in public libraries. Many people feel that doing this goes against their freedom of speech. Another problem with banning books is that, even among people who believe it is okay to ban books, what some people feel should be banned, others do not. For example, some people feel the *Harry Potter* books should be banned because of the witchcraft in them. Others think these books are fine but that any books that mention sex should be banned. Even some of history's most loved and respected books are among those that some people feel should be banned. To this day, Mark Twain's *The Adventures of Huckleberry Finn* remains near the top of the list of books that some people try to ban from schools.

Some of the 50 Most Challenged Books, 1990–2000	
A Wrinkle in Time by Madeleine L'Engle	*Huckleberry Finn* by Mark Twain
*Alice** by Phyllis Reynolds Naylor	*Of Mice and Men* by John Steinbeck
*Anastasia Krupnik** by Lois Lowry	*Scary Stories** by Alvin Schwartz
Blubber by Judy Blume	*The Catcher in the Rye* by J.D. Salinger
Deenie by Judy Blume	*The Color Purple* by Alice Walker
Forever by Judy Blume	*The Giver* by Lois Lowry
*Goosebumps** by R. L. Stine	*The Outsiders* by S.E. Hinton
Halloween ABC by Eve Merriam	*The Witches* by Roald Dahl
*Harry Potter** by J. K. Rowling	*To Kill a Mockingbird* by Harper Lee

*series of books

Questions to Ponder

1. What does it mean if something is banned?
2. What guarantees a person's freedom of speech in the U.S.?
3. What does "effective" mean?
4. Name two writers who have more than one book among the 50 most challenged between 1990–2000.
5. You may have read a book that has been banned somewhere at some time. Are there any books you've read you think *should* be banned? Do you think *any* books should be banned or restricted?

Not Just a Wide Street

There are many streets in the world named "Broadway," but the most famous one runs through the middle of New York City. It is older than the United States itself, dating back to the early 17th century. But Broadway is famous for another reason: theater.

❖❖❖It's a Fact!❖❖❖

Harold Prince has won more Tonys than anyone: 20. His wins include eight as a director, 10 as a producer, and two special awards.

"They say the neon lights are bright on Broadway" are the first words to a classic song—and pretty much everyone knows what the singer is talking about. If a play or musical is being produced (put on) on Broadway or an actor gets work in one of these plays, that's as big as it gets in the world of theater. Each year, the major awards for theater, the Tony Awards, honor plays and musicals produced on Broadway, as well as the people in them. The Tony Awards have been given since 1947. The awards ceremony has been televised nationally since 1967. There are currently 22 award categories, including awards for directing, acting, and music. Many movie stars have won Tony Awards, including Matthew Broderick, Kevin Spacey, Glenn Close, Nathan Lane, Laurence Fishburne, Al Pacino, Ingrid Bergman, and John Lithgow. The most important awards, however, are Best Play and Best Musical. Several of the winners in these categories have later been made into famous films, including *Biloxi Blues*, *Annie*, *Amadeus*, *Evita*, *The Miracle Worker*, *My Fair Lady*, and *The Sound of Music*. In recent years, however, some winners have come from the movies, such as *The Lion King*.

Most Tony Awards, Best Play

#	Playwright	Plays (Year)
3	Tom Stoppard	*Rosencrantz and Guildenstern Are Dead* (1968), *Travesties* (1976), *The Real Thing* (1984)
2	Arthur Miller*	*Death of a Salesman* (1949), *The Crucible* (1953)
	Edward Albee	*Who's Afraid of Virginia Woolf?* (1963), *Edward Albee's The Goat or Who Is Sylvia?* (2002)
	Peter Shaffer	*Equus* (1975), *Amadeus* (1981)
	Neil Simon	*Biloxi Blues* (1985), *Lost in Yonkers* (1991)
	Tony Kushner	*Angels in America: Millennium Approaches* (1993), *Angels in America: Perestroika* (1994)
	Terrence McNally	*Love! Valour! Compassion!* (1995), *Master Class* (1996)

*also won Best Author for *All My Sons* in 1947, when no Best Play award was given

Questions to Ponder

1. Where is the world's most famous street named Broadway?

2. What does a Broadway producer do?

3. Who wrote plays that won Best Play two years in a row?

4. Which play won Best Play at the 30th Annual Tony Awards?

5. If you worked in the theater world, would you like to work on Broadway, where there is a lot of pressure for plays to be successful; or would you rather work off-Broadway, where the plays can be just as good but there is not as much focus on money? Explain your answer.

Better Ways to Listen

The invention of the gramophone by Emile Berliner in 1887 allowed people to record and buy recordings of music. Think of it: before then, no one had ever heard music in any way other than at a live performance! As you can imagine, people loved this new technology, and in no time records (the simple name given to these recordings) were extremely popular. Still, by today's standards the technology was primitive. The sound quality wasn't great, and the record players weren't very convenient to use. It wasn't until about the middle of the 20th century that long-playing records (LPs) were for sale.

These records (LPs and the shorter "singles") were the only ways to buy recorded music until the middle of the 1960s. It was then that eight-track tapes were developed. These became popular as a new format in which to listen to music—and the first in which people could listen in the car (other than by radio)—but records remained popular. At the end of the '70s this changed with the introduction of the cassette tape—which could also be played in cars. Cassettes were much smaller than records. Also, records could be scratched easily, while cassettes could not. Cassettes also gave rise to a new way to hear music: the portable cassette player. People could now go for a walk while listening to a favorite album. Records began to sell less as cassettes became popular.

Then came the compact disc. This format was clearly better than anything before. Because it uses laser technology and only light touches the CD itself while playing, CDs do not wear out like cassettes and records. Also, CDs do not scratch easily, and they're portable (so you can listen to them at home, while walking, and while driving around). Additionally, the sound quality is *much* better than that of cassettes and albums, and you can easily skip from song to song. CDs were introduced in the mid 1980s, and since then they have come to be by far the favorite format. Records and cassettes have become harder and harder to find because companies don't make them as much. They know that most of us want CDs! The way we listen to music has been changed forever.

Sales of Recorded Music by Format (in millions)

Format	1992	1993	1994	1995	1996	1997	1998	1999	2000	2001
compact disc	407.5	495.4	662.1	722.9	778.9	753.1	847.0	938.9	942.5	881.9
CD single	7.3	7.8	9.3	21.5	43.2	66.7	56.0	55.9	34.2	17.3
cassette	366.4	339.5	345.4	272.6	225.3	172.6	158.5	123.6	76.0	45.0
cassette single	84.6	85.6	81.1	70.7	59.9	42.2	26.4	14.2	1.3	0
LP/EP (vinyl)	2.3	1.2	1.9	2.2	2.9	2.7	3.4	2.9	2.2	2.3
vinyl single	19.8	15.1	11.7	10.2	10.1	7.5	5.4	5.3	4.8	5.5

Questions to Ponder

1. What was the first way in which people could listen to music (aside from a live performance)?

2. Name two ways in which CDs were an improvement over both records and cassettes.

3. Which format has sold fewer copies every year since 1993?

4. What happened to the sales of vinyl records in 2001 that was different from what happened to all other forms of recorded music?

5. Think about how the ways in which people watch movies have changed over the years. Do you see any similarities between this and what's happened with the way we listen to music? Support your answer.

Keeping Parents Informed

There has been a rating system for movies since 1966. However, since television is something in our homes and it is on all the time, it gets watched more than movies get seen. Even so, there had never been any kind of rating system for TV to let people know about the content of programs (what's in them) so they could decide if there are shows they might want to avoid. This was considered particularly important for parents, because they are the ones responsible for what their children watch—and so the guidelines would help them keep their children from watching things that they felt were not appropriate for kids.

Finally, in 1997, most of the TV industry agreed to add labels to most of their programs. There were two parts to the guidelines. One was simply four letters that referred to what's in the program: D (for *dialog* that some people might consider offensive), L (bad *language*), S (*sex*), and V (*violence*). The second part of the guidelines is a rating system for shows like the one for movies (see below). These guidelines suggest to parents what programs are appropriate for which age groups. Parents can even buy TVs that will block out programs with certain ratings unless a code is entered into the TV to let that program be shown. This way, parents can keep their kids from watching certain kinds of programs—even when the parents are not around to do it themselves!

TV Parental Guidelines

The following icons appear in the upper left corner of the picture frame for the first 15 seconds of a program. If the program is longer than one hour, the icon should be repeated at the beginning of the second hour.

TV Y	This program is designed to be appropriate for all children.
TV Y7	This program is designed for children age 7 and above.
TV G	Most parents would find this program suitable for all ages.
TV PG	This program contains material that parents may find unsuitable for younger children.
TV 14	This program contains some material that many parents would find unsuitable for children under 14 years of age.
TV MA	This program is specifically designed to be viewed by adults and therefore may be unsuitable for children under 17.

Questions to Ponder

1. What in the TV guidelines lets you know that a show contains violence?

2. How long were there movie ratings before there were ones for TV?

3. How many categories for TV shows might parents of an 11-year-old particularly want to avoid? What are they?

4. If a TV show is two hours long, how many times will you see the show's rating, and where and when will you see it?

5. Many people do not like the TV guidelines. They feel that labeling shows is dangerous to our freedom because some people think certain kinds of shows are bad—and then some TV networks are afraid to run those shows. Do you agree or disagree with this? Why or why not?

Numbers and Statistics

92806
49849
52778
92820
75401
44627

NEW YORK STOCK EXCHANGE

AAR		4.16	-.02	+.25
ABB Ltd		2.88	+.19	+.66
ABM s .38f	2.8	13.51	-.24	+.27
ABN Amro .93e	5.6	16.47	+1.02	+1.67
ABN pfA 1.88	7.4	25.56	-.06	-.22
ABN pfB 1.78	6.9	25.76	+.11	-.10
ACE Cap 2.22	8.5	26.27	-.08	+.02
ACE Ltd .68	2.2	30.34	+1.87	+3.74
ACE pfl 4.19	7.0	58.60	+1.98	+4.64
ACM Op .72	7.9	9.14	+.05	-.04
ACM Inco .87	10.3	8.46	+.07	-.05
ACMMD .81	11.4	7.08	+.12	-.30
ACM MI .51	10.8	4.73	+.03	...
ACMMu .87	7.7	11.23	-.01	...
AES Cp		3.31	+.09	+.19
AES pfC 3.38	16.5	20.45	+.36	+1.51
AFLAC .28f	.8	33.36	+.39	+1.86
AGCO		17.28	+.93	+2.18
AGL Cap pf 2.00	7.5	26.71	+.13	+.96
AGL Res 1.08	4.6	23.40	+.31	+.90

1950 **2000** **2050**

55858
60402
44947
33109
62806

What's Inside . . . .

THE WORLD ALMANAC The Perpetual Calendar

Every January 1 we begin using a new calendar for the new year. The new calendar will help us plan our weeks and months. For example, do you need to know what day of the week your birthday will fall on this year? The calendar will help you. What many people don't realize, though, is that it's fairly simple to tell what day of the week your birthday will fall on 10 years from now, or 20, or 200. The perpetual calendar is the tool that helps you to do this.

The principle behind the perpetual calendar is very simple: there are only seven days on which a new year can begin—Sunday, Monday, Tuesday, etc. Once you know which day that is, the rest of the year is set because the lengths of the months are always the same: there are always 31 days in March, 30 in April, etc. The one exception is February, which is 29 days long once every four years (a leap year), and 28 days the rest of the time. What does all of this add up to? That there are only 14 possible ways in which the days of the week can be arranged for a year: seven for non-leap years, and seven for leap years. A perpetual calendar is a layout of these 14 possibilities. (See the chart below and on page 63.) Once you determine which of the 14 possible calendars applies to a given year—for which you need to know only what day of the week January 1 was for that year, and if that year is a leap year—you can easily find out the layout of the calendar for any year. "Perpetual" means lasting forever, repeating—and so you can see, since you can always use this calendar and since it applies to every possible year, how it got its name!

Match the number of the calendar (1–14) to the year in the table below. For example, the year 2000 followed the 14th calendar. The year 2010 will follow the 6th calendar.

1821....2	1847....6	1873....4	1899....1	1925....5	1951....2	1977....7	2003....4	2029....2	2055....6
1822....3	1848...14	1874....5	1900....2	1926....6	1952...10	1978....1	2004...12	2030....3	2056...14
1823....4	1849....2	1875....6	1901....3	1927....7	1953....5	1979....2	2005....7	2031....4	2057....2
1824...12	1850....3	1876...14	1902....4	1928....8	1954....6	1980...10	2006....1	2032...12	2058....3
1825....7	1851....4	1877....2	1903....5	1929....3	1955....7	1981....5	2007....2	2033....7	2059....4
1826....1	1852...12	1878....3	1904...13	1930....4	1956....8	1982....6	2008...10	2034....1	2060...12
1827....2	1853....7	1879....4	1905....1	1931....5	1957....3	1983....7	2009....5	2035....2	2061....7
1828...10	1854....1	1880...12	1906....2	1932...13	1958....4	1984....8	2010....6	2036...10	2062....1
1829....5	1855....2	1881....7	1907....3	1933....1	1959....5	1985....3	2011....7	2037....5	2063....2
1830....6	1856...10	1882....1	1908...11	1934....2	1960...13	1986....4	2012....8	2038....6	2064...10
1831....7	1857....5	1883....2	1909....6	1935....3	1961....1	1987....5	2013....3	2039....7	2065....5
1832....8	1858....6	1884...10	1910....7	1936...11	1962....2	1988...13	2014....4	2040....8	2066....6
1833....3	1859....7	1885....5	1911....1	1937....6	1963....3	1989....1	2015....5	2041....3	2067....7
1834....4	1860....8	1886....6	1912....9	1938....7	1964...11	1990....2	2016...13	2042....4	2068....8
1835....5	1861....3	1887....7	1913....4	1939....1	1965....6	1991....3	2017....1	2043....5	2069....3
1836...13	1862....4	1888....8	1914....5	1940....9	1966....7	1992...11	2018....2	2044...13	2070....4
1837....1	1863....5	1889....3	1915....6	1941....4	1967....1	1993....6	2019....3	2045....1	2071....5
1838....2	1864...13	1890....4	1916...14	1942....5	1968....9	1994....7	2020...11	2046....2	2072...13
1839....3	1865....1	1891....5	1917....2	1943....6	1969....4	1995....1	2021....6	2047....3	2073....1
1840...11	1866....2	1892...13	1918....3	1944...14	1970....5	1996....9	2022....7	2048...11	2074....2
1841....6	1867....3	1893....1	1919....4	1945....2	1971....6	1997....4	2023....1	2049....6	2075....3
1842....7	1868...11	1894....2	1920...12	1946....3	1972...14	1998....5	2024....9	2050....7	2076...11
1843....1	1869....6	1895....3	1921....7	1947....4	1973....2	1999....6	2025....4	2051....1	2077....6
1844....9	1870....7	1896...11	1922....1	1948...12	1974....3	2000...14	2026....5	2052....9	2078....7
1845....4	1871....1	1897....6	1923....2	1949....7	1975....4	2001....2	2027....6	2053....4	2079....1
1846....5	1872....9	1898....7	1924...10	1950....1	1976...12	2002....3	2028...14	2054....5	2080....9

1

JANUARY

S	M	T	W	T	F	S
1	2	3	4	5	6	7
8	9	10	11	12	13	14
15	16	17	18	19	20	21
22	23	24	25	26	27	28
29	30	31				

MAY

S	M	T	W	T	F	S
	1	2	3	4	5	6
7	8	9	10	11	12	13
14	15	16	17	18	19	20
21	22	23	24	25	26	27
28	29	30	31			

SEPTEMBER

S	M	T	W	T	F	S
					1	2
3	4	5	6	7	8	9
10	11	12	13	14	15	16
17	18	19	20	21	22	23
24	25	26	27	28	29	30

FEBRUARY

S	M	T	W	T	F	S
			1	2	3	4
5	6	7	8	9	10	11
12	13	14	15	16	17	18
19	20	21	22	23	24	25
26	27	28				

JUNE

S	M	T	W	T	F	S
				1	2	3
4	5	6	7	8	9	10
11	12	13	14	15	16	17
18	19	20	21	22	23	24
25	26	27	28	29	30	

OCTOBER

S	M	T	W	T	F	S
1	2	3	4	5	6	7
8	9	10	11	12	13	14
15	16	17	18	19	20	21
22	23	24	25	26	27	28
29	30	31				

MARCH

S	M	T	W	T	F	S
			1	2	3	4
5	6	7	8	9	10	11
12	13	14	15	16	17	18
19	20	21	22	23	24	25
26	27	28	29	30	31	

JULY

S	M	T	W	T	F	S
						1
2	3	4	5	6	7	8
9	10	11	12	13	14	15
16	17	18	19	20	21	22
23	24	25	26	27	28	29
30	31					

NOVEMBER

S	M	T	W	T	F	S
			1	2	3	4
5	6	7	8	9	10	11
12	13	14	15	16	17	18
19	20	21	22	23	24	25
26	27	28	29	30		

APRIL

S	M	T	W	T	F	S
						1
2	3	4	5	6	7	8
9	10	11	12	13	14	15
16	17	18	19	20	21	22
23	24	25	26	27	28	29
30						

AUGUST

S	M	T	W	T	F	S
		1	2	3	4	5
6	7	8	9	10	11	12
13	14	15	16	17	18	19
20	21	22	23	24	25	26
27	28	29	30	31		

DECEMBER

S	M	T	W	T	F	S
					1	2
3	4	5	6	7	8	9
10	11	12	13	14	15	16
17	18	19	20	21	22	23
24	25	26	27	28	29	30
31						

2

JANUARY

S	M	T	W	T	F	S
	1	2	3	4	5	6
7	8	9	10	11	12	13
14	15	16	17	18	19	20
21	22	23	24	25	26	27
28	29	30	31			

MAY

S	M	T	W	T	F	S
		1	2	3	4	5
6	7	8	9	10	11	12
13	14	15	16	17	18	19
20	21	22	23	24	25	26
27	28	29	30	31		

SEPTEMBER

S	M	T	W	T	F	S
						1
2	3	4	5	6	7	8
9	10	11	12	13	14	15
16	17	18	19	20	21	22
23	24	25	26	27	28	29
30						

FEBRUARY

S	M	T	W	T	F	S
				1	2	3
4	5	6	7	8	9	10
11	12	13	14	15	16	17
18	19	20	21	22	23	24
25	26	27	28			

JUNE

S	M	T	W	T	F	S
					1	2
3	4	5	6	7	8	9
10	11	12	13	14	15	16
17	18	19	20	21	22	23
24	25	26	27	28	29	30

OCTOBER

S	M	T	W	T	F	S
	1	2	3	4	5	6
7	8	9	10	11	12	13
14	15	16	17	18	19	20
21	22	23	24	25	26	27
28	29	30	31			

MARCH

S	M	T	W	T	F	S
				1	2	3
4	5	6	7	8	9	10
11	12	13	14	15	16	17
18	19	20	21	22	23	24
25	26	27	28	29	30	31

JULY

S	M	T	W	T	F	S
1	2	3	4	5	6	7
8	9	10	11	12	13	14
15	16	17	18	19	20	21
22	23	24	25	26	27	28
29	30	31				

NOVEMBER

S	M	T	W	T	F	S
				1	2	3
4	5	6	7	8	9	10
11	12	13	14	15	16	17
18	19	20	21	22	23	24
25	26	27	28	29	30	

APRIL

S	M	T	W	T	F	S
1	2	3	4	5	6	7
8	9	10	11	12	13	14
15	16	17	18	19	20	21
22	23	24	25	26	27	28
29	30					

AUGUST

S	M	T	W	T	F	S
			1	2	3	4
5	6	7	8	9	10	11
12	13	14	15	16	17	18
19	20	21	22	23	24	25
26	27	28	29	30	31	

DECEMBER

S	M	T	W	T	F	S
						1
2	3	4	5	6	7	8
9	10	11	12	13	14	15
16	17	18	19	20	21	22
23	24	25	26	27	28	29
30	31					

3

JANUARY

S	M	T	W	T	F	S
		1	2	3	4	5
6	7	8	9	10	11	12
13	14	15	16	17	18	19
20	21	22	23	24	25	26
27	28	29	30	31		

MAY

S	M	T	W	T	F	S
			1	2	3	4
5	6	7	8	9	10	11
12	13	14	15	16	17	18
19	20	21	22	23	24	25
26	27	28	29	30	31	

SEPTEMBER

S	M	T	W	T	F	S
1	2	3	4	5	6	7
8	9	10	11	12	13	14
15	16	17	18	19	20	21
22	23	24	25	26	27	28
29	30					

FEBRUARY

S	M	T	W	T	F	S
					1	2
3	4	5	6	7	8	9
10	11	12	13	14	15	16
17	18	19	20	21	22	23
24	25	26	27	28		

JUNE

S	M	T	W	T	F	S
						1
2	3	4	5	6	7	8
9	10	11	12	13	14	15
16	17	18	19	20	21	22
23	24	25	26	27	28	29
30						

OCTOBER

S	M	T	W	T	F	S
		1	2	3	4	5
6	7	8	9	10	11	12
13	14	15	16	17	18	19
20	21	22	23	24	25	26
27	28	29	30	31		

MARCH

S	M	T	W	T	F	S
					1	2
3	4	5	6	7	8	9
10	11	12	13	14	15	16
17	18	19	20	21	22	23
24	25	26	27	28	29	30
31						

JULY

S	M	T	W	T	F	S
	1	2	3	4	5	6
7	8	9	10	11	12	13
14	15	16	17	18	19	20
21	22	23	24	25	26	27
28	29	30	31			

NOVEMBER

S	M	T	W	T	F	S
					1	2
3	4	5	6	7	8	9
10	11	12	13	14	15	16
17	18	19	20	21	22	23
24	25	26	27	28	29	30

APRIL

S	M	T	W	T	F	S
	1	2	3	4	5	6
7	8	9	10	11	12	13
14	15	16	17	18	19	20
21	22	23	24	25	26	27
28	29	30				

AUGUST

S	M	T	W	T	F	S
				1	2	3
4	5	6	7	8	9	10
11	12	13	14	15	16	17
18	19	20	21	22	23	24
25	26	27	28	29	30	31

DECEMBER

S	M	T	W	T	F	S
1	2	3	4	5	6	7
8	9	10	11	12	13	14
15	16	17	18	19	20	21
22	23	24	25	26	27	28
29	30	31				

4 2003

JANUARY

S	M	T	W	T	F	S
			1	2	3	4
5	6	7	8	9	10	11
12	13	14	15	16	17	18
19	20	21	22	23	24	25
26	27	28	29	30	31	

MAY

S	M	T	W	T	F	S
				1	2	3
4	5	6	7	8	9	10
11	12	13	14	15	16	17
18	19	20	21	22	23	24
25	26	27	28	29	30	31

SEPTEMBER

S	M	T	W	T	F	S
	1	2	3	4	5	6
7	8	9	10	11	12	13
14	15	16	17	18	19	20
21	22	23	24	25	26	27
28	29	30				

FEBRUARY

S	M	T	W	T	F	S
						1
2	3	4	5	6	7	8
9	10	11	12	13	14	15
16	17	18	19	20	21	22
23	24	25	26	27	28	

JUNE

S	M	T	W	T	F	S
1	2	3	4	5	6	7
8	9	10	11	12	13	14
15	16	17	18	19	20	21
22	23	24	25	26	27	28
29	30					

OCTOBER

S	M	T	W	T	F	S
			1	2	3	4
5	6	7	8	9	10	11
12	13	14	15	16	17	18
19	20	21	22	23	24	25
26	27	28	29	30	31	

MARCH

S	M	T	W	T	F	S
						1
2	3	4	5	6	7	8
9	10	11	12	13	14	15
16	17	18	19	20	21	22
23	24	25	26	27	28	29
30	31					

JULY

S	M	T	W	T	F	S
		1	2	3	4	5
6	7	8	9	10	11	12
13	14	15	16	17	18	19
20	21	22	23	24	25	26
27	28	29	30	31		

NOVEMBER

S	M	T	W	T	F	S
						1
2	3	4	5	6	7	8
9	10	11	12	13	14	15
16	17	18	19	20	21	22
23	24	25	26	27	28	29
30						

APRIL

S	M	T	W	T	F	S
		1	2	3	4	5
6	7	8	9	10	11	12
13	14	15	16	17	18	19
20	21	22	23	24	25	26
27	28	29	30			

AUGUST

S	M	T	W	T	F	S
					1	2
3	4	5	6	7	8	9
10	11	12	13	14	15	16
17	18	19	20	21	22	23
24	25	26	27	28	29	30
31						

DECEMBER

S	M	T	W	T	F	S
	1	2	3	4	5	6
7	8	9	10	11	12	13
14	15	16	17	18	19	20
21	22	23	24	25	26	27
28	29	30	31			

5

JANUARY

S	M	T	W	T	F	S
				1	2	3
4	5	6	7	8	9	10
11	12	13	14	15	16	17
18	19	20	21	22	23	24
25	26	27	28	29	30	31

MAY

S	M	T	W	T	F	S
					1	2
3	4	5	6	7	8	9
10	11	12	13	14	15	16
17	18	19	20	21	22	23
24	25	26	27	28	29	30
31						

SEPTEMBER

S	M	T	W	T	F	S
		1	2	3	4	5
6	7	8	9	10	11	12
13	14	15	16	17	18	19
20	21	22	23	24	25	26
27	28	29	30			

FEBRUARY

S	M	T	W	T	F	S
1	2	3	4	5	6	7
8	9	10	11	12	13	14
15	16	17	18	19	20	21
22	23	24	25	26	27	28

JUNE

S	M	T	W	T	F	S
	1	2	3	4	5	6
7	8	9	10	11	12	13
14	15	16	17	18	19	20
21	22	23	24	25	26	27
28	29	30				

OCTOBER

S	M	T	W	T	F	S
				1	2	3
4	5	6	7	8	9	10
11	12	13	14	15	16	17
18	19	20	21	22	23	24
25	26	27	28	29	30	31

MARCH

S	M	T	W	T	F	S
1	2	3	4	5	6	7
8	9	10	11	12	13	14
15	16	17	18	19	20	21
22	23	24	25	26	27	28
29	30	31				

JULY

S	M	T	W	T	F	S
			1	2	3	4
5	6	7	8	9	10	11
12	13	14	15	16	17	18
19	20	21	22	23	24	25
26	27	28	29	30	31	

NOVEMBER

S	M	T	W	T	F	S
1	2	3	4	5	6	7
8	9	10	11	12	13	14
15	16	17	18	19	20	21
22	23	24	25	26	27	28
29	30					

APRIL

S	M	T	W	T	F	S
			1	2	3	4
5	6	7	8	9	10	11
12	13	14	15	16	17	18
19	20	21	22	23	24	25
26	27	28	29	30		

AUGUST

S	M	T	W	T	F	S
						1
2	3	4	5	6	7	8
9	10	11	12	13	14	15
16	17	18	19	20	21	22
23	24	25	26	27	28	29
30	31					

DECEMBER

S	M	T	W	T	F	S
		1	2	3	4	5
6	7	8	9	10	11	12
13	14	15	16	17	18	19
20	21	22	23	24	25	26
27	28	29	30	31		

6

JANUARY

S	M	T	W	T	F	S
					1	2
3	4	5	6	7	8	9
10	11	12	13	14	15	16
17	18	19	20	21	22	23
24	25	26	27	28	29	30
31						

MAY

S	M	T	W	T	F	S
						1
2	3	4	5	6	7	8
9	10	11	12	13	14	15
16	17	18	19	20	21	22
23	24	25	26	27	28	29
30	31					

SEPTEMBER

S	M	T	W	T	F	S
			1	2	3	4
5	6	7	8	9	10	11
12	13	14	15	16	17	18
19	20	21	22	23	24	25
26	27	28	29	30		

FEBRUARY

S	M	T	W	T	F	S
	1	2	3	4	5	6
7	8	9	10	11	12	13
14	15	16	17	18	19	20
21	22	23	24	25	26	27
28						

JUNE

S	M	T	W	T	F	S
		1	2	3	4	5
6	7	8	9	10	11	12
13	14	15	16	17	18	19
20	21	22	23	24	25	26
27	28	29	30			

OCTOBER

S	M	T	W	T	F	S
					1	2
3	4	5	6	7	8	9
10	11	12	13	14	15	16
17	18	19	20	21	22	23
24	25	26	27	28	29	30
31						

MARCH

S	M	T	W	T	F	S
	1	2	3	4	5	6
7	8	9	10	11	12	13
14	15	16	17	18	19	20
21	22	23	24	25	26	27
28	29	30	31			

JULY

S	M	T	W	T	F	S
				1	2	3
4	5	6	7	8	9	10
11	12	13	14	15	16	17
18	19	20	21	22	23	24
25	26	27	28	29	30	31

NOVEMBER

S	M	T	W	T	F	S
	1	2	3	4	5	6
7	8	9	10	11	12	13
14	15	16	17	18	19	20
21	22	23	24	25	26	27
28	29	30				

APRIL

S	M	T	W	T	F	S
				1	2	3
4	5	6	7	8	9	10
11	12	13	14	15	16	17
18	19	20	21	22	23	24
25	26	27	28	29	30	

AUGUST

S	M	T	W	T	F	S
1	2	3	4	5	6	7
8	9	10	11	12	13	14
15	16	17	18	19	20	21
22	23	24	25	26	27	28
29	30	31				

DECEMBER

S	M	T	W	T	F	S
			1	2	3	4
5	6	7	8	9	10	11
12	13	14	15	16	17	18
19	20	21	22	23	24	25
26	27	28	29	30	31	

The Perpetual Calendar *(cont.)*

7 2005

JANUARY							MAY							SEPTEMBER						
S	M	T	W	T	F	S	S	M	T	W	T	F	S	S	M	T	W	T	F	S
						1	1	2	3	4	5	6	7					1	2	3
2	3	4	5	6	7	8	8	9	10	11	12	13	14	4	5	6	7	8	9	10
9	10	11	12	13	14	15	15	16	17	18	19	20	21	11	12	13	14	15	16	17
16	17	18	19	20	21	22	22	23	24	25	26	27	28	18	19	20	21	22	23	24
23	24	25	26	27	28	29	29	30	31					25	26	27	28	29	30	
30	31																			
FEBRUARY							JUNE							OCTOBER						
S	M	T	W	T	F	S	S	M	T	W	T	F	S	S	M	T	W	T	F	S
		1	2	3	4	5				1	2	3	4							1
6	7	8	9	10	11	12	5	6	7	8	9	10	11	2	3	4	5	6	7	8
13	14	15	16	17	18	19	12	13	14	15	16	17	18	9	10	11	12	13	14	15
20	21	22	23	24	25	26	19	20	21	22	23	24	25	16	17	18	19	20	21	22
27	28						26	27	28	29	30			23	24	25	26	27	28	29
														30	31					
MARCH							JULY							NOVEMBER						
S	M	T	W	T	F	S	S	M	T	W	T	F	S	S	M	T	W	T	F	S
		1	2	3	4	5						1	2			1	2	3	4	5
6	7	8	9	10	11	12	3	4	5	6	7	8	9	6	7	8	9	10	11	12
13	14	15	16	17	18	19	10	11	12	13	14	15	16	13	14	15	16	17	18	19
20	21	22	23	24	25	26	17	18	19	20	21	22	23	20	21	22	23	24	25	26
27	28	29	30	31			24	25	26	27	28	29	30	27	28	29	30			
							31													
APRIL							AUGUST							DECEMBER						
S	M	T	W	T	F	S	S	M	T	W	T	F	S	S	M	T	W	T	F	S
					1	2		1	2	3	4	5	6					1	2	3
3	4	5	6	7	8	9	7	8	9	10	11	12	13	4	5	6	7	8	9	10
10	11	12	13	14	15	16	14	15	16	17	18	19	20	11	12	13	14	15	16	17
17	18	19	20	21	22	23	21	22	23	24	25	26	27	18	19	20	21	22	23	24
24	25	26	27	28	29	30	28	29	30	31				25	26	27	28	29	30	31

8

JANUARY							MAY							SEPTEMBER						
S	M	T	W	T	F	S	S	M	T	W	T	F	S	S	M	T	W	T	F	S
1	2	3	4	5	6	7			1	2	3	4	5							1
8	9	10	11	12	13	14	6	7	8	9	10	11	12	2	3	4	5	6	7	8
15	16	17	18	19	20	21	13	14	15	16	17	18	19	9	10	11	12	13	14	15
22	23	24	25	26	27	28	20	21	22	23	24	25	26	16	17	18	19	20	21	22
29	30	31					27	28	29	30	31			23	24	25	26	27	28	29
														30						
FEBRUARY							JUNE							OCTOBER						
S	M	T	W	T	F	S	S	M	T	W	T	F	S	S	M	T	W	T	F	S
			1	2	3	4						1	2		1	2	3	4	5	6
5	6	7	8	9	10	11	3	4	5	6	7	8	9	7	8	9	10	11	12	13
12	13	14	15	16	17	18	10	11	12	13	14	15	16	14	15	16	17	18	19	20
19	20	21	22	23	24	25	17	18	19	20	21	22	23	21	22	23	24	25	26	27
26	27	28	29				24	25	26	27	28	29	30	28	29	30	31			
MARCH							JULY							NOVEMBER						
S	M	T	W	T	F	S	S	M	T	W	T	F	S	S	M	T	W	T	F	S
				1	2	3	1	2	3	4	5	6	7					1	2	3
4	5	6	7	8	9	10	8	9	10	11	12	13	14	4	5	6	7	8	9	10
11	12	13	14	15	16	17	15	16	17	18	19	20	21	11	12	13	14	15	16	17
18	19	20	21	22	23	24	22	23	24	25	26	27	28	18	19	20	21	22	23	24
25	26	27	28	29	30	31	29	30	31					25	26	27	28	29	30	
APRIL							AUGUST							DECEMBER						
S	M	T	W	T	F	S	S	M	T	W	T	F	S	S	M	T	W	T	F	S
1	2	3	4	5	6	7				1	2	3	4							1
8	9	10	11	12	13	14	5	6	7	8	9	10	11	2	3	4	5	6	7	8
15	16	17	18	19	20	21	12	13	14	15	16	17	18	9	10	11	12	13	14	15
22	23	24	25	26	27	28	19	20	21	22	23	24	25	16	17	18	19	20	21	22
29	30						26	27	28	29	30	31		23	24	25	26	27	28	29
														30	31					

9

JANUARY							MAY							SEPTEMBER						
S	M	T	W	T	F	S	S	M	T	W	T	F	S	S	M	T	W	T	F	S
	1	2	3	4	5	6				1	2	3	4	1	2	3	4	5	6	7
7	8	9	10	11	12	13	5	6	7	8	9	10	11	8	9	10	11	12	13	14
14	15	16	17	18	19	20	12	13	14	15	16	17	18	15	16	17	18	19	20	21
21	22	23	24	25	26	27	19	20	21	22	23	24	25	22	23	24	25	26	27	28
28	29	30	31				26	27	28	29	30	31		29	30					
FEBRUARY							JUNE							OCTOBER						
S	M	T	W	T	F	S	S	M	T	W	T	F	S	S	M	T	W	T	F	S
				1	2	3							1			1	2	3	4	5
4	5	6	7	8	9	10	2	3	4	5	6	7	8	6	7	8	9	10	11	12
11	12	13	14	15	16	17	9	10	11	12	13	14	15	13	14	15	16	17	18	19
18	19	20	21	22	23	24	16	17	18	19	20	21	22	20	21	22	23	24	25	26
25	26	27	28	29			23	24	25	26	27	28	29	27	28	29	30	31		
							30													
MARCH							JULY							NOVEMBER						
S	M	T	W	T	F	S	S	M	T	W	T	F	S	S	M	T	W	T	F	S
					1	2		1	2	3	4	5	6						1	2
3	4	5	6	7	8	9	7	8	9	10	11	12	13	3	4	5	6	7	8	9
10	11	12	13	14	15	16	14	15	16	17	18	19	20	10	11	12	13	14	15	16
17	18	19	20	21	22	23	21	22	23	24	25	26	27	17	18	19	20	21	22	23
24	25	26	27	28	29	30	28	29	30	31				24	25	26	27	28	29	30
31																				
APRIL							AUGUST							DECEMBER						
S	M	T	W	T	F	S	S	M	T	W	T	F	S	S	M	T	W	T	F	S
	1	2	3	4	5	6					1	2	3	1	2	3	4	5	6	7
7	8	9	10	11	12	13	4	5	6	7	8	9	10	8	9	10	11	12	13	14
14	15	16	17	18	19	20	11	12	13	14	15	16	17	15	16	17	18	19	20	21
21	22	23	24	25	26	27	18	19	20	21	22	23	24	22	23	24	25	26	27	28
28	29	30					25	26	27	28	29	30	31	29	30	31				

10

JANUARY							MAY							SEPTEMBER						
S	M	T	W	T	F	S	S	M	T	W	T	F	S	S	M	T	W	T	F	S
		1	2	3	4	5					1	2	3		1	2	3	4	5	6
6	7	8	9	10	11	12	4	5	6	7	8	9	10	7	8	9	10	11	12	13
13	14	15	16	17	18	19	11	12	13	14	15	16	17	14	15	16	17	18	19	20
20	21	22	23	24	25	26	18	19	20	21	22	23	24	21	22	23	24	25	26	27
27	28	29	30	31			25	26	27	28	29	30	31	28	29	30				
FEBRUARY							JUNE							OCTOBER						
S	M	T	W	T	F	S	S	M	T	W	T	F	S	S	M	T	W	T	F	S
					1	2	1	2	3	4	5	6	7				1	2	3	4
3	4	5	6	7	8	9	8	9	10	11	12	13	14	5	6	7	8	9	10	11
10	11	12	13	14	15	16	15	16	17	18	19	20	21	12	13	14	15	16	17	18
17	18	19	20	21	22	23	22	23	24	25	26	27	28	19	20	21	22	23	24	25
24	25	26	27	28	29		29	30						26	27	28	29	30	31	
MARCH							JULY							NOVEMBER						
S	M	T	W	T	F	S	S	M	T	W	T	F	S	S	M	T	W	T	F	S
						1			1	2	3	4	5							1
2	3	4	5	6	7	8	6	7	8	9	10	11	12	2	3	4	5	6	7	8
9	10	11	12	13	14	15	13	14	15	16	17	18	19	9	10	11	12	13	14	15
16	17	18	19	20	21	22	20	21	22	23	24	25	26	16	17	18	19	20	21	22
23	24	25	26	27	28	29	27	28	29	30	31			23	24	25	26	27	28	29
30	31													30						
APRIL							AUGUST							DECEMBER						
S	M	T	W	T	F	S	S	M	T	W	T	F	S	S	M	T	W	T	F	S
		1	2	3	4	5						1	2		1	2	3	4	5	6
6	7	8	9	10	11	12	3	4	5	6	7	8	9	7	8	9	10	11	12	13
13	14	15	16	17	18	19	10	11	12	13	14	15	16	14	15	16	17	18	19	20
20	21	22	23	24	25	26	17	18	19	20	21	22	23	21	22	23	24	25	26	27
27	28	29	30				24	25	26	27	28	29	30	28	29	30	31			
							31													

11

JANUARY							MAY							SEPTEMBER						
S	M	T	W	T	F	S	S	M	T	W	T	F	S	S	M	T	W	T	F	S
			1	2	3	4						1	2			1	2	3	4	5
5	6	7	8	9	10	11	3	4	5	6	7	8	9	6	7	8	9	10	11	12
12	13	14	15	16	17	18	10	11	12	13	14	15	16	13	14	15	16	17	18	19
19	20	21	22	23	24	25	17	18	19	20	21	22	23	20	21	22	23	24	25	26
26	27	28	29	30	31		24	25	26	27	28	29	30	27	28	29	30			
							31													
FEBRUARY							JUNE							OCTOBER						
S	M	T	W	T	F	S	S	M	T	W	T	F	S	S	M	T	W	T	F	S
						1		1	2	3	4	5	6					1	2	3
2	3	4	5	6	7	8	7	8	9	10	11	12	13	4	5	6	7	8	9	10
9	10	11	12	13	14	15	14	15	16	17	18	19	20	11	12	13	14	15	16	17
16	17	18	19	20	21	22	21	22	23	24	25	26	27	18	19	20	21	22	23	24
23	24	25	26	27	28	29	28	29	30					25	26	27	28	29	30	31
MARCH							JULY							NOVEMBER						
S	M	T	W	T	F	S	S	M	T	W	T	F	S	S	M	T	W	T	F	S
1	2	3	4	5	6	7				1	2	3	4	1	2	3	4	5	6	7
8	9	10	11	12	13	14	5	6	7	8	9	10	11	8	9	10	11	12	13	14
15	16	17	18	19	20	21	12	13	14	15	16	17	18	15	16	17	18	19	20	21
22	23	24	25	26	27	28	19	20	21	22	23	24	25	22	23	24	25	26	27	28
29	30	31					26	27	28	29	30	31		29	30					
APRIL							AUGUST							DECEMBER						
S	M	T	W	T	F	S	S	M	T	W	T	F	S	S	M	T	W	T	F	S
			1	2	3	4							1			1	2	3	4	5
5	6	7	8	9	10	11	2	3	4	5	6	7	8	6	7	8	9	10	11	12
12	13	14	15	16	17	18	9	10	11	12	13	14	15	13	14	15	16	17	18	19
19	20	21	22	23	24	25	16	17	18	19	20	21	22	20	21	22	23	24	25	26
26	27	28	29	30			23	24	25	26	27	28	29	27	28	29	30	31		
							30	31												

12 2004

JANUARY							MAY							SEPTEMBER						
S	M	T	W	T	F	S	S	M	T	W	T	F	S	S	M	T	W	T	F	S
				1	2	3							1				1	2	3	4
4	5	6	7	8	9	10	2	3	4	5	6	7	8	5	6	7	8	9	10	11
11	12	13	14	15	16	17	9	10	11	12	13	14	15	12	13	14	15	16	17	18
18	19	20	21	22	23	24	16	17	18	19	20	21	22	19	20	21	22	23	24	25
25	26	27	28	29	30	31	23	24	25	26	27	28	29	26	27	28	29	30		
							30	31												
FEBRUARY							JUNE							OCTOBER						
S	M	T	W	T	F	S	S	M	T	W	T	F	S	S	M	T	W	T	F	S
1	2	3	4	5	6	7			1	2	3	4	5						1	2
8	9	10	11	12	13	14	6	7	8	9	10	11	12	3	4	5	6	7	8	9
15	16	17	18	19	20	21	13	14	15	16	17	18	19	10	11	12	13	14	15	16
22	23	24	25	26	27	28	20	21	22	23	24	25	26	17	18	19	20	21	22	23
29							27	28	29	30				24	25	26	27	28	29	30
														31						
MARCH							JULY							NOVEMBER						
S	M	T	W	T	F	S	S	M	T	W	T	F	S	S	M	T	W	T	F	S
	1	2	3	4	5	6					1	2	3		1	2	3	4	5	6
7	8	9	10	11	12	13	4	5	6	7	8	9	10	7	8	9	10	11	12	13
14	15	16	17	18	19	20	11	12	13	14	15	16	17	14	15	16	17	18	19	20
21	22	23	24	25	26	27	18	19	20	21	22	23	24	21	22	23	24	25	26	27
28	29	30	31				25	26	27	28	29	30	31	28	29	30				
APRIL							AUGUST							DECEMBER						
S	M	T	W	T	F	S	S	M	T	W	T	F	S	S	M	T	W	T	F	S
				1	2	3	1	2	3	4	5	6	7				1	2	3	4
4	5	6	7	8	9	10	8	9	10	11	12	13	14	5	6	7	8	9	10	11
11	12	13	14	15	16	17	15	16	17	18	19	20	21	12	13	14	15	16	17	18
18	19	20	21	22	23	24	22	23	24	25	26	27	28	19	20	21	22	23	24	25
25	26	27	28	29	30		29	30	31					26	27	28	29	30	31	

13

JANUARY							MAY							SEPTEMBER						
S	M	T	W	T	F	S	S	M	T	W	T	F	S	S	M	T	W	T	F	S
					1	2	1	2	3	4	5	6	7					1	2	3
3	4	5	6	7	8	9	8	9	10	11	12	13	14	4	5	6	7	8	9	10
10	11	12	13	14	15	16	15	16	17	18	19	20	21	11	12	13	14	15	16	17
17	18	19	20	21	22	23	22	23	24	25	26	27	28	18	19	20	21	22	23	24
24	25	26	27	28	29	30	29	30	31					25	26	27	28	29	30	
31																				
FEBRUARY							JUNE							OCTOBER						
S	M	T	W	T	F	S	S	M	T	W	T	F	S	S	M	T	W	T	F	S
	1	2	3	4	5	6				1	2	3	4							1
7	8	9	10	11	12	13	5	6	7	8	9	10	11	2	3	4	5	6	7	8
14	15	16	17	18	19	20	12	13	14	15	16	17	18	9	10	11	12	13	14	15
21	22	23	24	25	26	27	19	20	21	22	23	24	25	16	17	18	19	20	21	22
28	29						26	27	28	29	30			23	24	25	26	27	28	29
														30	31					
MARCH							JULY							NOVEMBER						
S	M	T	W	T	F	S	S	M	T	W	T	F	S	S	M	T	W	T	F	S
		1	2	3	4	5						1	2			1	2	3	4	5
6	7	8	9	10	11	12	3	4	5	6	7	8	9	6	7	8	9	10	11	12
13	14	15	16	17	18	19	10	11	12	13	14	15	16	13	14	15	16	17	18	19
20	21	22	23	24	25	26	17	18	19	20	21	22	23	20	21	22	23	24	25	26
27	28	29	30	31			24	25	26	27	28	29	30	27	28	29	30			
							31													
APRIL							AUGUST							DECEMBER						
S	M	T	W	T	F	S	S	M	T	W	T	F	S	S	M	T	W	T	F	S
					1	2		1	2	3	4	5	6					1	2	3
3	4	5	6	7	8	9	7	8	9	10	11	12	13	4	5	6	7	8	9	10
10	11	12	13	14	15	16	14	15	16	17	18	19	20	11	12	13	14	15	16	17
17	18	19	20	21	22	23	21	22	23	24	25	26	27	18	19	20	21	22	23	24
24	25	26	27	28	29	30	28	29	30	31				25	26	27	28	29	30	31

14

JANUARY							MAY							SEPTEMBER						
S	M	T	W	T	F	S	S	M	T	W	T	F	S	S	M	T	W	T	F	S
						1		1	2	3	4	5	6						1	2
2	3	4	5	6	7	8	7	8	9	10	11	12	13	3	4	5	6	7	8	9
9	10	11	12	13	14	15	14	15	16	17	18	19	20	10	11	12	13	14	15	16
16	17	18	19	20	21	22	21	22	23	24	25	26	27	17	18	19	20	21	22	23
23	24	25	26	27	28	29	28	29	30	31				24	25	26	27	28	29	30
30	31																			
FEBRUARY							JUNE							OCTOBER						
S	M	T	W	T	F	S	S	M	T	W	T	F	S	S	M	T	W	T	F	S
		1	2	3	4	5					1	2	3	1	2	3	4	5	6	7
6	7	8	9	10	11	12	4	5	6	7	8	9	10	8	9	10	11	12	13	14
13	14	15	16	17	18	19	11	12	13	14	15	16	17	15	16	17	18	19	20	21
20	21	22	23	24	25	26	18	19	20	21	22	23	24	22	23	24	25	26	27	28
27	28	29					25	26	27	28	29	30		29	30	31				
MARCH							JULY							NOVEMBER						
S	M	T	W	T	F	S	S	M	T	W	T	F	S	S	M	T	W	T	F	S
			1	2	3	4							1				1	2	3	4
5	6	7	8	9	10	11	2	3	4	5	6	7	8	5	6	7	8	9	10	11
12	13	14	15	16	17	18	9	10	11	12	13	14	15	12	13	14	15	16	17	18
19	20	21	22	23	24	25	16	17	18	19	20	21	22	19	20	21	22	23	24	25
26	27	28	29	30	31		23	24	25	26	27	28	29	26	27	28	29	30		
							30	31												
APRIL							AUGUST							DECEMBER						
S	M	T	W	T	F	S	S	M	T	W	T	F	S	S	M	T	W	T	F	S
						1			1	2	3	4	5						1	2
2	3	4	5	6	7	8	6	7	8	9	10	11	12	3	4	5	6	7	8	9
9	10	11	12	13	14	15	13	14	15	16	17	18	19	10	11	12	13	14	15	16
16	17	18	19	20	21	22	20	21	22	23	24	25	26	17	18	19	20	21	22	23
23	24	25	26	27	28	29	27	28	29	30	31			24	25	26	27	28	29	30
30														31						

Questions to Ponder

1. If there were no such thing as leap years, how many possible calendar layouts would there be?
2. What is a principle?
3. Using the perpetual calendar above, what day of the week will it be on Christmas Day in 2020?
4. Looking only at January 1 through February 28, what is the difference between the seven non-leap year calendars and the seven leap year calendars? Why do you think this is?
5. What are some ways in which you might find the perpetual calendar useful?

Who Is Dow Jones?

In 1882, Charles Dow and Henry Jones, two financial reporters, formed Dow Jones & Company, Inc., and they began publishing a newsletter about the performance of the New York Stock Exchange (NYSE). Eventually this newsletter grew into *The Wall Street Journal*, which is now considered to be the world's leading business publication. So that's the "who." However, when people today talk about "the Dow Jones" (or sometimes just "the Dow"), they are not talking about these two men but about something called the Dow Jones Industrial Average (DJIA), which is the most well-known measure of how the NYSE is doing.

◆◆◆It's a Fact!◆◆◆

The Great Depression started when the New York Stock Exchange crashed (suddenly went down in value a great deal) beginning on October 29, 1929. By July of 1932, the value of the Dow had dropped by 89%. It did not recover until the 1940s.

The NYSE is where people can buy and sell shares (small parts) of the companies that are part of it (currently about 3,000 companies). Everyone who holds shares in a company is a part-owner of that company—and the more shares they own, the more of the company they own. Shares are traded (bought and sold) based on points, which translate directly into dollars and cents. For example, if one share in a company is being traded for 2.25 points, it costs $2.25.

The DJIA is the average value of 30 of the biggest companies traded on the NYSE multiplied by 200, and this is the main way that the performance of NYSE is measured. Each of these 30 companies is called a component of the Dow. Here's a simplified model of how it all works: Let's pretend that the DJIA has three components instead of 30—call them Companies A, B, and C. When the NYSE opens on Monday morning, shares of Company A are trading for 4.50, B for 4.70, and C for 5.80, and so the Dow at that point stands at 1,000.00—the result of [(A + B + C) /3] x 200. During the week many shares are bought and sold, and so the prices of the shares go up and down. At the end of the week, A is trading for 4.30, B for 6.45, and C for 5.75—and so now the Dow is 1,100.00. Based on this, we can say that the Dow rose 100 points over the course of the week. The "average" in the DJIA also refers to the average percentage change of the 30 DJIA stocks. In our mini-example, the DJIA rose 10% for the week.

Who Is Dow Jones? *(cont.)*

There are many companies in the New York Stock Exhange other than the 30 which make up the DJIA, and how an individual company does is not directly tied to how the DJIA does. But the idea is that the 30 companies—which at present (because they do change from time to time) range from American Express and General Motors to McDonald's and Disney—are different enough that they give a general picture of how the NYSE as a whole is doing. So the next time you hear someone say, "The stock market rose 150 points today," you'll know what they're talking about!

Components of the Dow Jones Industrial Average (as of Dec. 20th, 2002)

Company (Stock Symbol)	Share Value
Aluminum Co. of America (AA)	23.85
American Express (AXP)	37.02
AT&T (T)	26.58
Boeing Co.(BA)	32.71
Caterpillar Inc. (CAT)	46.50
Citigroup Inc. (C)	38.14
Coca-Cola Co. (KO)	44.08
DuPont (DD)	42.96
Eastman Kodak (EK)	36.41
Exxon Mobil Corp. (XOM)	35.70
General Electric (GE)	25.95
General Motors (GM)	37.06
Honeywell Int'l. Inc. (HON)	23.53
Hewlett-Packard Co. (HPQ)	18.91
Home Depot (HD)	24.83
Intel Corp. (INTC)	17.01
International Business Machines (IBM)	79.79
International Paper (IP)	35.33
J.P. Morgan (JPM)	24.87
Johnson & Johnson (JNJ)	54.52
McDonald's Corp. (MCD)	15.75
Merck & Co. (MRK)	56.36
Microsoft (MSFT)	53.04
Minnesota Mining/Mfg. (MMM)	124.13
Philip Morris Cos. (MO)	41.12
Procter & Gamble (PG)	87.68
SBC Communications (SBC)	28.21
United Technologies (UTX)	62.11
Wal-Mart Stores Inc. (WMT)	50.79
Walt Disney Co. (DIS)	16.46
	Total: 8511.32

Questions to Ponder

1. From where does the Dow Jones get its name?
2. How many companies are components of the DJIA?
3. There are many stock markets in the world. Which one does the DJIA have to do with?
4. If on Dec, 20, 2002, you bought 23 shares of KO, how much would it have cost?
5. What company would you most like to be a part owner of, even if it's just a very small part? Why do you choose that company?

Keeping Track

The earliest record of a census dates back to ancient Babylon in 3800 B.C.E, and it was taken as a way to estimate how much money would be received in taxes. Ancient China, Egypt, and Greece also took censuses, but it was not until the Roman Empire that census-taking became something done regularly. The Romans used their censuses to see how they should tax their inhabitants and how many men in a given area could be drafted into the military. The responsibility for census-taking fell to local census-takers, who also collected taxes.

In the 17th century, Sweden was the first country to try to get a truly accurate count of its inhabitants. What is considered the first modern census (that is to say, one that took more detailed information about the people it counted) was taken in a French African colony in 1665. The U.S. census of 1790 was the first to make its information public. It is written into the Constitution that the U.S. must take a census every 10 years (which is the standard for census-taking around the world), and information gathered from that first census was used to know how to pay back individual states for their expenses in helping to fight Britain in the Revolutionary War. It contained just six questions: the name of the head of the household, the number of free white males 16 or older, the number of free white males under 16, the number of free white females, the number of other free persons, and the number of slaves. In 1790, 17 marshals (and the assistants they hired as needed) were in charge of the U.S. census, and all information had to be taken down by hand.

✧✧✧It's a Fact!✧✧✧

The U.S. Census Bureau also conducts censuses of agriculture, state and local governments, and various industries every five years, as well special censuses for the government when needed.

By the mid 19th century, printed census forms were in use, and soon the number and scope of the questions were expanded. In 1890 the U.S. began using simple punch-card machines to help record the data, and in 1902 the Census Bureau was formed. Today, the Census Bureau employs almost 1 million people (though many of them for only a short time around census time) and uses computers to record and analyze all of the information gathered (most of which is done via mail), which can be as many as 60 questions per census form. Collecting this information helps the government to better manage programs of energy, transportation, health care, emergency services, and so forth, because it shows them a big picture of how many people live where, and what their lives are like.

Questions to Ponder

1. When is it considered that the first modern census was taken?
2. Generally, how often is a census taken?
3. Was census-taking first done by the Romans? Explain your answer.
4. If there are about 300 million people living in the United States, about what percentage of them are working for the Census Bureau around census time?
5. If you were putting together a census but could ask only three questions, what would they be? Explain why you think the answers to these questions are especially important to have.

Exchanging Money for Money

In 2002, 12 of the 15 countries that belong to the European Union (EU) switched from their separate national units of currency to a common unit: the euro. (Denmark, Sweden, and the United Kingdom did not.) The process of changing over to a new monetary unit was a massive version of something that happens every day: the exchange of one kind of money for another. People can do this at banks, airports, or certain shops that exist just to change money; and governments deal with this every time they buy, sell, or trade goods with each other.

The rates of foreign exchange (the process of exchanging one type of money for another) are constantly changing. This is based on the purchasing power of a country's currency, or how much of something a certain amount of that currency will buy. For example, let's say a certain type of car made in Japan costs $20,000 in the U.S. Switzerland does not use the U.S. dollar, of course, but Swiss franc, and so that same Japanese car will cost almost 30,000 francs. This is because the purchasing power of one U.S. dollar is equal to about one-and-a-half Swiss francs. That same car will cost somewhat over 600 dinars in Kuwait, because one Kuwaiti dinar is equal to about U.S. $3.25. This does not mean that U.S. dollars are better than Swiss francs or worse that Kuwaiti dinars, just that different countries have different basic units of money on which their currencies are based. After all, if you had to do the same amount of work to earn two dollars as you did for one dinar, which would you rather be paid? But the rates of exchange between countries change every day. Basically, this happens because the strength of countries' economies varies. While Japan may sell that car in the U.S. for $20,000 today, if a month later the U.S. economy is a little weaker and the Japanese economy has grown a little stronger and nothing else has changed, it will take a few more dollars to buy that same car.

Sample Rates of Exchange

Country	Monetary Unit	= U.S. $1	Country	Monetary Unit	= U.S. $1
Australia	dollar	.7843	Israel	shekel	.2936
Brazil	real	.9402	Japan	yen	.007900
Canada	dollar	.7207	Kuwait	dinar	3.2841
China	renminbi	.1201	Mexico	peso	.1258
European Union	euro	1.047	Russia	ruble	.0001739
Hong Kong	dollar	.1291	South Africa	rand	.2249
India	rupee	.02796	Switzerland	franc	.6800

═══ Questions to Ponder ═══

1. What is the process of trading one kind of money for another called?

2. If you are an American traveling in Japan, why can't you just use the money you use at home?

3. If the U.S. economy becomes weaker over a year while the Russian economy stays the same, what will this probably mean in terms of exchanging dollars for rubles?

4. According to the table above, how many Canadian dollars would you get for U.S. $500? How many would you get for 500 Mexican pesos? (Round to the hundredths place.)

5. Most countries in the EU now use a common currency. Name two good and two bad things you think might come from countries giving up their own currencies and agreeing on a common one.

The Electoral College

The United States is a democracy. That means that the people elect their government officials. What many Americans don't realize is that, when it comes to the two highest governmental positions in the U.S., the people do not vote for them directly; instead, it is done indirectly through the electoral college.

During a presidential election, Americans cast what is called a popular vote for the candidates they would like to see be president and vice-president for the next four years. However, the votes they cast are actually for electors. Each state and the District of Columbia get to send as many electors to the electoral college as they have senators (two for every state) plus representatives (the larger a state's population, the more representatives it has) in Congress. For example, Wyoming is the least-populous state, and it has only one representative (every state gets at least one)—so it sends three electors to the electoral college. The college meets on the first Monday after the second Wednesday in the December after a presidential election.

In most states, the political party whose candidates win the popular vote in that state gets to choose its electors. Currently, the only states that do this differently are Maine and Nebraska, where parties choose electors based on the percentage of the popular vote they get. (For example, if Maine's popular vote is evenly split between the Democrat and the Republican candidates, each party gets to choose two electors.) Electors are free to vote for whomever they want, but they almost always vote for their party's candidates.

Some people think the electoral college is not a good idea, since it makes it possible for a person to become president who does not win the popular vote. This has happened four times so far: John Q. Adams, Rutherford B. Hayes, Benjamin Harrison, and George W. Bush all became president despite receiving fewer popular votes than their opponents.

Electoral Votes by State

Questions to Ponder

1. When does the electoral college meet?
2. Which state sends the most electors to the electoral college? How many?
3. What is the fewest number of electoral votes a state can have?
4. If Democrats get 54% of New York's popular vote in a presidential election and Republicans get 46%, how many electors do the Republicans get to choose?
5. Do you think the United States should continue to use the electoral college, even though people do not directly choose their two highest governmental officials? Explain your answer.

The Cost of Living, Then and Now

"A dollar doesn't buy what it used to." Have you ever heard anyone say something like this? Well, it's true—but not for the reasons they may have in mind. You see, as years go by, the prices of things go up, as does the amount of money people earn at work. So, naturally, what someone could buy for a dollar 50 years ago is not what they can buy now for the same amount. But there's a way to figure out exactly how the value of money changes: the consumer price index (CPI). The CPI is a way of measuring the changes in the prices of goods and services over time. To calculate the CPI, you choose a reference year— for example, 1970. Then you select a range of basic

> ◊◊◊**It's a Fact!**◊◊◊
>
> The U.S. Bureau of Labor Statistics began keeping the CPI during World War I. They did this because shortages forced the prices of many things to increase very rapidly, and so a way was needed for companies to know how much more they needed to pay their workers to keep them earning enough money to live.

goods and services which consumers (people who buy and use things) in general need to have for their day-to-day living: food, shelter, clothing, charges for doctors' services, etc. After you've found the combined cost of these things, you divide the total by whatever number you need so that the result is 100 (the number used to represent $1 in the CPI). So, if the combined cost is $20,000, you would simply divide this by itself: $20,000 divided by $20,000 equals $1, or 100. Then you do the same thing for the year that you want to compare to your reference year—except that instead of dividing the combined cost by itself, you divide it by $20,000. Let's say your comparison year is 1980, and the combined cost of the range of goods and services for that year is $30,000. In this case, you divide $30,000 by $20,000. Your answer is $1.50, or 150. What this tells you is that what cost $1 in 1970 cost $1.50 in 1980. Why would anyone need to know this? What good is the CPI? Well, the CPI gives businesses some idea of how much the cost of living changes over time. In turn, this gives them some idea of how much they need to increase the pay of their employees so that those employees can keep their jobs and be able to make enough money to live as the prices of things rise.

Consumer Price Index, 1915–2002 (Reference year: 1967 (100))

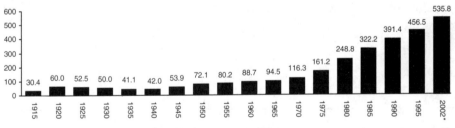

Questions to Ponder

1. Why doesn't a dollar buy as much as now as it did 50 years ago?

2. What is a consumer?

3. Would souvenirs bought while on vacation be covered in the range of things that are used to determine the CPI? Why or why not?

4. According to the CPI, how much more did it cost to live in 1990 than it did in 1940? (Express your answer as a percentage.)

5. Name five things not mentioned in the article that you think need to be among the goods and services that make up the CPI, and explain why each should be included.

Who's Watching What

Television shows live and die by one statistic: ratings. For each episode of every show, TV networks try to determine approximately how many people watched. The networks have no direct way of knowing who you are and what shows you watch, so how do they know who's watching what? The answer (in the United States, anyway) is something you've probably heard of: the Nielsen ratings.

The A. C. Nielsen Company has been taking surveys of how many people tune in to shows since the 1930s. That was before television, and the surveys were done for radio shows. Once television came to be, Nielsen continued to do their surveys. What people are watching is recorded in two ways: people write down what they watch (in what are called diaries), and boxes that record what shows people watch are attached to some TVs.

There are too many homes and TVs in the country for Nielsen to keep track of what everybody is watching. What they do instead is randomly select a *representative sampling* of the population to take part in their surveys. This means that they do their best to get a smaller group of people, the breakdown of which is just like the breakdown of society as a whole. For example, if 13% of the U.S. is made up of white males between the ages of 25–34, then Nielsen will make sure that 13% of their survey group is made up of the same sub-group, or *demographic*. The idea is that the TV-watching habits of society as a whole are reflected in the Nielsen surveys. The Nielsen ratings are simply the results of these surveys. The highest-rated show is the one which the largest percentage of TVs in the country are tuned to.

All-Time Highest-Rated TV Programs

Program	Date	Network	Rating %	Households
1. *M*A*S*H* (last episode)	2/28/83	CBS	60.2	50.15 million
2. *Dallas* ("Who Shot J.R.?")	11/21/80	CBS	53.3	41.47 million
3. *Roots* (pt. 8)	1/30/77	ABC	51.1	36.38 million
4. Super Bowl XVI	1/24/82	CBS	49.1	40.02 million
5. Super Bowl XVII	1/30/83	NBC	48.6	40.48 million
6. XVII Winter Olympics (2nd Wed.)	2/23/94	CBS	48.5	45.69 million
7. Super Bowl XX	1/26/86	NBC	48.3	41.49 million
8. *Gone with the Wind* (pt. 1)	11/7/76	NBC	47.7	33.96 million
9. *Gone with the Wind* (pt. 2)	11/8/76	NBC	47.4	33.75 million
10. Super Bowl XII	1/15/78	CBS	47.2	34.41 million

Questions to Ponder

1. Since there are too many people to keep track of what all of them are watching, what does the A. C. Nielsen Company do to estimate the viewing-habits of the country as a whole?

2. What does "to determine" mean?

3. What show has appeared four times among the ten all-time highest-rated programs?

4. Looking at the list above, you can see that more households watched the #6 show than watched the #2 show. How can a show with 45.69 million households watching it have a lower rating percentage than a show with over four million less?

5. Name two benefits and two drawbacks of the system that Nielsen uses to rank TV shows.

The Zoning Improvement Program

Anyone who's ever sent or received a letter in the United States knows what that five-digit code is that comes after the state: the zip code, of course, the last part of the address. Right? Well, yes . . . and no. First of all, it's actually ZIP—an acronym for "Zoning Improvement Program." Second, it isn't really part of your address; and technically, you do not have to use it. But today it's such a part of everyday life in the U.S. that it's okay to write "zip code"—and probably not a good idea to mail a letter without one!

The Zoning Improvement Program was introduced in 1963 as a way to make it simpler for the U.S. Postal Service to distribute mail throughout the country. The first digit, from 0 to 9, indicates one of 10 major geographical areas in the U.S., each one of these areas consisting of at least three states. Within these areas, each state is divided into an average of 10 smaller areas, which are identified by the second and third digits. The fourth and fifth digits identify a post office or local delivery area. For example, take the ZIP Code 92831: "9" means the West Coast—California, Oregon, Washington, Alaska, or Hawaii; "28" means a particular

> ❖❖❖**It's a Fact!**❖❖❖
>
> In 1983, the U.S. Postal Service began its "ZIP + 4" program, adding four digits to all ZIP codes—for example, 92831-2359 to help further simplify its delivery process. The "+ 4" are voluntary—although using them can be good for business: some businesses that send large quantities of mail get discounts for using the ZIP + 4.

northern part of Orange County (the entire county currently ranges from "06" to "28"); "3" means the city of Fullerton; and "1" means a particular part of Fullerton. But it's important to keep in mind that each number is affected by the number before it. The ZIP Code 82831 is Arvada, Wyoming—and so the "3" here obviously doesn't mean Fullerton, California!

ZIP Code Map, 10 Major Areas

Questions to Ponder

1. When were ZIP Codes introduced?

2. What is the minimum number of states in each of the 10 major geographical ZIP Code areas?

3. What is an acronym?

4. If you were mailing a letter from California to Kentucky, what would be the first number of the Zip Code? What about if you were mailing it from New York?

5. The ZIP Code is used only in the U.S. Many other countries have similar codes, often called "postal codes." Do you think it would be better if all countries used the same postal code? What problems might there be with this? What benefits?

$\mathcal{S}ports$

What's Inside . . . .

Trophies of the NHL

All sports bestow honors to both the individuals and teams who rise above their peers and help to define athletic excellence. But perhaps no sports organization can boast as rich a history when it comes to its awards as the National Hockey League (NHL).

Stanley Cup (championship trophy)—The roots of the Stanley Cup extend back to 1892, making it the oldest trophy competed for by professional athletes in North America. But it's not just the Cup's age that makes it special. Did you know that the Stanley Cup is the only professional sports trophy on which the name of every member of the winning team is inscribed? (As you can imagine, this takes up quite a bit of space! Sometimes, bands of names have to be removed and retired.) Also, if you are a member of the winning team, you get to take the Cup home with you for one whole day. This unique tradition allows everyone—from the superstar goal scorer to the equipment manager—an opportunity to be a part of the trophy's lore.

➠**Past Winners (# of trophies won):** Montreal Canadians 23; Toronto Maple Leafs 13

Hart Memorial Trophy—Each year, every major team sport honors one player by presenting him or her with an MVP (Most Valuable Player) trophy. In the NHL, that trophy is called the Hart Memorial Trophy. The original trophy was donated to the NHL by Dr. David Hart, whose son, Cecil Hart, went on to coach the Montreal Canadians to two Stanley Cup championships. The recipient of that first Hart Trophy was Frank Nighbor, who starred for Ottawa in the 1923–1924 season.

➠**Past recipients (# of trophies awarded):** Wayne Gretzky (9), Gordie Howe (6), Eddie Shore (4)

Lady Byng Memorial Trophy—It is not often that a major sporting trophy is named after a person who was not a player, coach, or administrator in that particular sport. Such is the case with the Lady Byng, which is given each year to the NHL player who exhibits the most gentlemanly conduct on the ice.

The award, named after the wife of Canada's Governor-General, was first awarded in 1925, to Frank Nighbor. The original trophy was eventually given permanently to Frank Boucher, who earned the trophy 7 times between 1928 and 1935. Every year since then, a replica is awarded to the player who displays both skill and sportsmanship.

➠**Past recipients (# of trophies won):** Frank Boucher (7), Wayne Gretzky (5), Red Kelly (4)

═══ Questions to Ponder ═══

1. Which team has won the most Stanley Cups?
2. Which hockey great was the first person awarded both the Hart Memorial Trophy and the Lady Byng Trophy?　a. Frank Boucher　　b. Frank Nighbor　　c. Wayne Gretzky
3. Frank Nighbor won the Hart Memorial Trophy while playing for Ottawa. Ottawa is the capital city of Canada. Complete this analogy: *Ottawa* is to *Canada* as _____ is to *United States of America*.
4. Hockey is the only major sport that awards "gentlemanly" play with a trophy. It is also the only team sport in which fistfights are a common and accepted part of almost every game. What is your opinion of this?
5. If you could create a new award that would be given for excellence in a particular sport or medium (music, television, movies, etc.), who would you name it after and who would be the first recipient of this award?

The World Plays Here

Basketball is played worldwide, but the United States has always been its hub. It was invented there and introduced to the world by the U.S. at the Olympics. However, it is the National Basketball Association (or NBA) that makes the U.S. the center of the basketball universe. For many years, the U.S. would not allow professionals on the U.S. Olympic team, instead fielding only their best college players. Even so, it won the gold medal in every Olympics from 1936 (the first year basketball was an official Olympic sport) through '68. They lost the gold-medal game in '72, but won again in '76 and '84 (not playing in '80 due to the U.S. Olympic boycott). And in '88, the U.S. won only the bronze. Then in '92 the U.S. changed policies and, like other nations, fielded a team of its very best players. The U.S. team so dominated that many called for the U.S. to go back to its old policy. It didn't, and the U.S. won gold in '96 and '00.

Meanwhile, the NBA was becoming more international. Beginning in the early 1980s, teams started showing an interest in foreign players. The first foreign-born NBA star was Nigerian Hakeem Olajuwon, drafted by the Houston Rockets in 1984. He went on to become one of the great centers in NBA history. Since then, the number of NBA players who call another country home has only increased. As of the 2002–'03 season, 35 countries and territories were represented by 67 players, including such stars as Dirk Nowitski (Germany), Pedrag Stojakovic (Greece), Steve Nash (Canada), Pau Gasol (Spain), and Yao Ming (China). Ironically, all of this may challenge U.S. Olympic dominance, since these non-American players improve in the NBA and then return to their home countries to play for their *own* Olympic teams. In other words, the internationalization of the NBA is helping the rest of the world to catch up.

2002 NBA Player Draft, First-Round Picks (Top 20)

Team	Player (Country)	Team	Player (Country)
1. Houston	Yao Ming (China)	11. Washington	Jared Jeffries (U.S.)
2. Chicago	Jay Williams (U.S.)	12. L.A. Clippers	Marvin Ely (U.S.)
3. Golden State	Mike Dunleavy (U.S.)	13. Milwaukee	Marcus Haislip (U.S.)
4. Memphis	Drew Gooden (U.S.)	14. Indiana	Fred Jones (U.S.)
5. Denver	Nikoloz Tskitishvili (Italy)	15. Houston	Bostjan Nachbar (Italy)
6. Cleveland	Dajuan Wagner (U.S.)	16. Philadelphia	Jiri Welsch (Slovenia)
7. New York	Maybyner Hilario (Brazil)	17. Washington	Juan Dixon (U.S.)
8. L.A. Clippers	Chris Wilcox (U.S.)	18. Orlando	Curtis Borchardt (U.S.)
9. Phoenix	Amare Stoudemire (U.S.)	19. Utah	Ryan Humphrey (U.S.)
10. Miami	Caron Butler (U.S.)	20. Toronto	Kareem Rush (U.S.)

Questions to Ponder

1. What percentage of the first 20 players drafted in 2002 were not Americans?

2. Which of the first 20 players come from the same foreign country, and what country is it?

3. Since basketball became an official Olympic sport, how many times has a team other than the U.S. won the gold medal? (Note: the Olympics were not held in 1940 and '44 because of WWII.)

4. What great foreign-born center was drafted by Houston in 1984? What country was he from?

5. Do you see any parallels between the internationalization of the NBA and the make up of the U.S. as a whole? Explain.

The Greatest

There have been many great boxers and many famous boxers. Muhammad Ali may or may not be the greatest boxer of them all, but there has never been one more famous. At one time Ali may have been the most famous person in the world, and the reasons go far beyond what he could do in the ring. And it is for these reasons as much as for his great boxing skills that Ali has always been known as "the Greatest."

Ali was known as Cassius Clay when he won an Olympic gold medal in 1960 and then the heavyweight championship of the world in 1964. Many people loved him because of his entertaining boxing style and his unique personality. However, shortly after becoming champion, he announced to the world that he had converted to the Islamic religion, and that he had taken a Muslim name: Muhammad Ali. Many people in society were upset by this, feeling that it was a rejection of society's rules. This suited Ali fine, because in one sense he *did* reject society—the part of society that was unfair and prejudiced. Ali has said that shortly after winning his gold medal he threw it in a river as a way of protesting racism in America.

> ◇◇◇**It's a Fact!**◇◇◇
>
> Muhammad Ali is the only person to ever win the heavyweight championship three separate times. He was champion from 1964 through 1967, when his title was taken away and he was stopped from boxing because of his refusal to be drafted into the military. He reclaimed the title in 1974 and held it until 1978. Later in 1978 after losing the title, he won it for the third time.

In the years to come, Ali was never shy about telling people what he believed and fighting to make the world a better place, refusing to act the way racists thought a black man should. He refused to take part in the military draft for the Vietnam War not only because he did not think it right for America to be in Vietnam, but also because he thought the way blacks were treated in the U.S. was wrong and so he didn't want to fight on the country's behalf. Because of this, his heavyweight championship was taken away from him, but Ali's principles were more important to him than any awards or titles.

As time went on, Ali boxed again, won the championship two more times and then eventually retired. Many changes did happen in society, and Ali became more and more loved. This was apparent in the 1996 Summer Olympics in Atlanta, when Ali, by now a middle-aged man with Parkinson's disease, was chosen to light the Olympic flame at the opening ceremonies and was cheered wildly by the whole country. People loved him for who he was and always had been—simply, the Greatest.

Questions to Ponder

1. What was Muhammad Ali's name at birth?
2. What religion did Ali convert to? When did he announce this?
3. What are a person's "principles"?
4. What are two things Ali did to protest racism in the U.S.?
5. Ali used his fame to do much more than make money. If you were famous, how do you think you would use that fame? Explain your answer.

The Bicycle Race

Although cycling is an Olympic event, by far the most popular bicycle race in the world is the Tour de France, sometimes simply called "the Tour." The race is held every July. As its name suggests, the Tour de France is a tour of France, winding across about 2,000 miles of French countryside. The course is different every year, and sometimes it goes through parts of neighboring countries such as Belgium, Spain, Germany, Switzerland, and England.

> ✧✧✧**It's a Fact!**✧✧✧
>
> The tradition of the *maillot jaune* was begun during the 1919 race as a way for the spectators to know who was leading the race.

The Tour is run in stages, or sections. There is usually a stage every day, and the race takes about a month to complete. Different stages involve different cycling skills, such as climbing hills or sprinting. Each rider is timed for each stage, and the person with the lowest cumulative (overall) time at the Tour's end is the winner. During the race, the person with the lowest cumulative time wears the *maillot jaune*, or yellow jersey.

The first Tour de France was held in 1903, and it has been held every year since, except for 1915–'18 because of World War I and 1940–'46 because of World War II. Over the course of the Tour, millions of spectators line much of the route. For the last stage alone—which always takes place at the famous Champs-Elysées of Paris—about a million show up to watch the winner cross the finish line.

Most Tour de France Victories

No.	Cyclist (Country); Years Won	No.	Cyclist (Country); Years Won
5	Miguel Indurain (Spain); 1991–'95	2	Lucien Petit-Breton (France); 1907–'08
	Jacques Anquetil (France); 1957, '61–'64		Firmin Lambot (Belgium); 1919, '22
	Eddy Merckx (Belgium); 1969–'72, '74		Ottavio Bottecchia (Italy); 1924–'25
	Bernard Hinault (France); 1978–'79, '81–'82, '85		Nicolas Frantz (Luxembourg); 1927–'28
4	Lance Armstrong (U.S.); 1999–2002		André Leducq (France); 1930, '32
3	Philippe Thys (Belgium); 1913–'14, '20		Antonin Magne (France); 1931, '34
	Louison Bobet (France); 1953–'55		Sylvère Maes (Belgium); 1936, '39
	Greg Lemond (U.S.); 1986, '89–'90		Gino Bartali (Italy); 1938, '48
			Fausto Coppi (Italy); 1949, '52
			Bernard Thévenet (France); 1975, '77
			Laurent Fignon (France); 1983–'84

Questions to Ponder

1. The course of the Tour de France changes every year, but in what city does it always end?

2. Who has won the second-most Tours in a row? How many?

3. Aside from the Tour de France, during what other event can you see bicycle racing?

4. What country has produced the highest percentage of multiple Tour de France winners? What is the percentage? (Round to the nearest whole percent.)

5. Imagine that you are a great athlete and are going to compete in the Tour. Explain the kind of training you would do to prepare for such a difficult race. (*Note:* "I would ride my bike a lot" is not a complete answer!)

The Triple Crown

In the world of horse racing, there is one achievement that stands above all others: winning the Triple Crown. This consists of winning the three biggest races in one year: the Kentucky Derby, the Preakness, and the Belmont Stakes.

The Triple Crown races are run by Thoroughbreds, a type of horse bred especially for its speed and strength. All modern Thoroughbreds are descended from at least one of three stallions (male horses over five years of age) imported to Great Britain from the Middle East and North Africa back between 1689 and 1724: the Byerly Turk, the Darley Arabian, and the Godolphin Barb. These horses were mated with strong English mares (female horses over five), and their offspring were both fast and could run for long distances.

> ### ◊◊◊It's a Fact!◊◊◊
> Thoroughbreds cost a great deal of money. This is in part because of how much prize money they can earn for their owners during their careers—they have earned as much as $6.5 million—but mostly because they can breed other Thoroughbreds, which in turn can make *more* money. The record paid for a Thoroughbred at auction is $30 million.

Horses in Triple Crown races must be three years old, and colts (males under five) must carry 126 pounds, while fillies (females under five) must carry 121. They are ridden by jockeys who are very small and light. If the jockeys weigh less than their horse's mandatory carry weight, lead bars are added to a pad underneath the saddle to make up the difference. All Triple Crown races are run on flat, oval tracks. The Kentucky Derby is 1¼ miles in length, the Preakness 1³⁄₁₆ miles, and the Belmont Stakes 1½ miles.

Triple Crown Winners

Year	Horse: Jockey; Trainer	Year	Horse: Jockey; Trainer
1919	Sir Barton: John Loftus; H. G. Bedwell	1946	Assault: Warren Mehrtens; Max Hirsch
1930	Gallant: Fox Earl Sande; Sunny Jim Fitzsimmons	1948	Citation: Eddie Arcaro; Jimmy Jones
1935	Omaha: William Saunders; Sunny Jim Fitzsimmons	1973	Secretariat: Ron Turcotte; Lucien Laurin
1937	War Admiral: Charles Kurtsinger; George Conway	1977	Seattle Slew: Jean Cruguet; Billy Turner
1941	Whirlaway: Eddie Arcaro; Ben Jones	1978	Affirmed: Steve Cauthen; Laz Barrera
1943	Count Fleet: John Longden; Don Cameron		

═══ Questions to Ponder ═══

1. What breed of horse competes in the Triple Crown races?
2. To what country can all Triple Crown-winning horses trace back their roots?
3. What is the combined length of the three Triple Crown races?
4. What is the oldest a Triple Crown winner has been? How do you know this?
5. The great jockey Johnny Longden, who died in 2003 at 96, had a great career as both jockey and trainer. Although he excelled at both, he said he enjoyed riding the most. If you could do only one of these activities, which would you choose? Why? Do you think it was the danger, the competition, or just the riding itself that led Longden to prefer being a jockey to being a trainer?

It's All About Speed

There are many different types of car races, from drag races that run just a quarter-mile to treks that cross entire countries. In the end, though, it's all about speed, about whose car covers the distance in the shortest amount of time. This idea is most easily seen in something that isn't actually a race: the pursuit of the land speed record.

Setting the land speed record is a simple idea: make your car go faster than anyone's ever has. Drivers have tried to set this record almost since the invention of the automobile. At the very beginning, some people thought that cars simply could not go faster than 30 miles per hour—and even that the skin on the driver's face would be ripped off at that speed! But soon cars were made to go faster and faster, and people stopped worrying about the limits, instead trying to push them. Soon cars were able to go over 100 mph, and in 1904 the Fédération Internationale de l'Automobile (FIA) was founded to be the governing body of motor sports—which means it is the organization that oversees all official sporting events in which cars compete. This includes attempts to set the land speed record. Today, attempts at the land speed record are run over the course of one mile. Cars make two runs of one mile apiece, and the top speeds reached during each run are averaged together. Beginning in the 1960s, rocket-powered cars replaced wheel-driven ones for record-setting attempts. In 1997, the speed of sound was broken by a car for the first—and, so far, only—time.

Land Speed Records by Decade

Date	Driver	Car	mph
4/29/1899	Jenatzy	*Jamais Contente*	65.792
1/26/1906	Marriott	Stanley	127.659
2/12/1919	DePalma	Packard	149.875
3/11/1929	Seagrave	Irving-Napier	231.446
8/23/1939	Cobb	Railton	368.9
9/16/1947	Cobb	Railton-Mobil	394.2
1950s	*(record not broken)*	***	***
11/15/1965	Breedlove	*Spirit of America*	600.601
10/23/1970	Gabelich	*Blue Flame*	622.407
10/9/1979	Barrett	*Budweiser Rocket*	638.637*
10/4/1983	Noble	*Thrust 2*	633.468
10/15/1997	Green	*Thrust SSC*	763.035

*not recognized as official by the FIA

Questions to Ponder

1. What are motor sports?
2. What is the last name of the first driver to go faster than 600 miles per hour?
3. What kind of car was used to break the speed of sound?
4. How many times faster was the land speed record set in the 1990s than the one set in the 1890s?
5. As you probably realize, trying to set the land speed record is very dangerous, and several people have died in the process. Do you think people should be allowed to try to set this record? Why or why not?

Comparing Pitchers

When a baseball team gets a win or a loss, so does a pitcher on that team. Because of this, wins and losses don't tell the whole story of how well pitchers do. Once a pitcher didn't give up a hit through 12 innings—but when he gave up a run in the 13th, he got the loss because his team hadn't scored any runs for him! People like strikeouts, but some of the best pitchers ever didn't strike out a lot of batters. Instead, it is earned-run average (ERA) that is the best way to evaluate how effective a pitcher is.

An unearned run is a run scored that is the product of an error by the other team in the field. These are not the fault of the pitching, and so unearned runs don't figure into a pitcher's ERA. And unlike wins and losses, how many runs a team scores for its pitcher doesn't have anything to do with ERA—because what does *that* have to do with how he's pitching? Nolan Ryan, one of the all-time greats, once ended a season with a record of 8 wins and 16 losses—but it wasn't his fault. The fact that he had the best ERA of any pitcher in the league that season showed this. A pitcher's ERA is simply the number of earned runs a pitcher allows *per nine innings* pitched. So, if at the end of a season a pitcher has pitched 270 innings and given up 90 earned runs, we first divide 90 by 270 to find out how many runs the pitcher allowed per inning. We then multiply that number (in this case, .333) by 9. We end up with 3.00, which is how many runs the pitcher has allowed per nine innings. (ERAs are always taken out to the hundredths place.)

This is a great way of comparing pitchers who are playing at the same time. However, it gets tricky when trying to compare pitchers of different eras, since various factors such as changes in rules and equipment affect how batters are able to hit. For example, in today's era, an ERA of 3.00 is pretty good. However, a pitcher with the same ERA between 1900 and 1920 wasn't doing so well. So, as in most sports, the statistics don't tell the whole story—even a statistic as useful as ERA!

Top Single-Season ERAs for Five Different Eras

ERA	Pitcher	Year	ERA	Pitcher	Year	ERA	Pitcher	Year
1900–'19			*1940–'59*			*1980–2002*		
0.96	Dutch Leonard	1914	1.64	Spud Chandler	1943	1.53	Dwight Gooden	1985
1.04	Three Fingers Brown	1906	1.78	Mort Cooper	1942	1.56	Greg Maddux	1994
1.14	Christy Mathewson	1909	1.81	Hal Newhouser	1945	1.63	Greg Maddux	1995
1.14	Walter Johnson	1913	1.90	Max Lanier	1943	1.69	Nolan Ryan	1981
1.15	Jack Pfiester	1907	1.94	Hal Newhouser	1946	1.74	Pedro Martinez	2000
1920–'39			*1960–'79*					
1.66	Carl Hubbell	1933	1.12	Bob Gibson	1968			
1.91	Pete Alexander	1920	1.60	Luis Tiant	1968			
1.93	Dolf Luque	1923	1.65	Dean Chance	1964			
2.00	Lon Warneke	1933	1.73	Sandy Koufax	1966			
2.06	Lefty Grove	1931	1.74	Sandy Koufax	1964			

Questions to Ponder

1. What is the benefit of using ERA as a way to evaluate pitchers?

2. What is an *era*?

3. In what 20-year period does it seem it was the hardest to score earned runs?

4. When Nolan Ryan went 8-16 in 1987, he gave up 65 earned runs in 211⅔ innings pitched. What was his league-leading ERA that year?

5. What is a way besides ERA that you think would be a good way to judge how good a pitcher is? Explain your answer.

The World's Fastest Human

In the world of competitive running, raw speed seems to thrill fans the most. The race that highlights this since the earliest track meets is the 100-meter dash. Whoever is the best in the world at this has always been considered "the world's fastest human."

Athletes who compete in the shortest running events are called sprinters, and they are like cheetahs in the animal kingdom: they run very fast over a very short distance. There are a few races that range between 50–200 meters, but 100 meters—which is long enough for a runner to reach maximum speed but short enough for that runner to maintain it—is the race by which "the world's fastest human" is determined. Many of the most famous track athletes of all time have run the 100 meters, including Jesse Owens and Carl Lewis. Women also run the 100 meters, but so far the title of the world's fastest human has always been held by a man.

As in most sports, every year track and field holds a championship, and whoever wins the 100 meters is the world champion for that year. However, by far the most popular track and field competition is held every four years at the Summer Olympics. Generally, the man who wins the 100 meters at the Olympics is the one considered the world's fastest human—even if someone has run the race faster that year. The title "the world's fastest human" is unofficial, though, so accuracy is not a big concern!

Men's 100 Meters Olympic Champions

Year	Gold-Medalist, Country	Time	Year	Gold-Medalist, Country	Time
1896	Thomas Burke, U.S.	12.0s	1956	Bobby Morrow, U.S.	10.5s
1900	Francis W. Jarvis, U.S.	11.0s	1960	Armin Mary, Germany	10.2s
1904	Archie Hahn, U.S.	11.0s	1964	Bob Hayes, U.S.	10.0s
1908	Reginald Walker, S. Africa	10.8s	1968	Jim Hines, U.S.	9.95s
1912	Ralph Craig, U.S.	10.8s	1972	Valery Borzov, U.S.S.R.	10.14s
1920	Charles Paddock, U.S.	10.8s	1976	Hasely Crawford, Trinidad	10.06s
1924	Harold Abrahams, G.B.	10.6s	1980	Allan Wells, G.B.	10.25s
1928	Percy Williams, Canada	10.8s	1984	Carl Lewis, U.S.	9.99s
1932	Eddie Tolan, U.S.	10.3s	1988	Carl Lewis, U.S.	9.92s
1936	Jesse Owens, U.S.	10.3s	1992	Linford Christie, G.B.	9.96s
1948	Harrison Dillard, U.S.	10.3s	1996	Donovan Bailey, Canada	9.84s
1952	Lindy Remigino, U.S.	10.4s	2000	Maurice Green, U.S.	9.87s

Questions to Ponder

1. Who is generally considered "the world's fastest human?"
2. Why is 100 meters the distance used to determine the world's fastest human?
3. Who holds the Olympic record for the 100 meters, and what is it?
4. The United States has won more Olympic 100 meters than any other country. What percent of the time has the U.S. won? (Round up to the nearest whole percent.)
5. The women's world record for the 100 meters is 10.49s. It was set by Florence Griffith Joyner in 1988. As you can see above, this time was good enough to have won the men's Olympic 100 meters until 1932, and again in 1956. Do you think a woman will ever be "the world's fastest human?" Why or why not?

The Biggest Sporting Event

In the United States, it's called soccer, but just about everywhere else it's called football, and it's been the world's most-popular sport for a very long time. Every four years, nations from all over the planet put together their best football teams and send them to the World Cup, an event that grabs the world's attention like no other.

In 1904, seven European countries formed the Fédération Internationale de Football Association (FIFA). It was put together with the idea of creating an international football tournament, but it wasn't until 1930, when it was decided that football outside of Europe had become good enough, that the first World Cup tournament was held. Just 13 teams took part. Today, however, nearly 200 countries participate. To cut down the number, qualifying rounds are held on each continent, and from there 32 teams advance to the World Cup tournament itself, the location of which changes each time. It takes nearly a month for a champion to emerge from the 32 teams, and during that time football fans from all over the world follow the tournament. It is estimated that the 1994 championship game had a TV audience of about one billion.

> ◇◇◇**It's a Fact!**◇◇◇
>
> Brazil's 1958, '62, and '70 teams were led by Pelé, who is generally considered the greatest player in World Cup history.

In 1991 the Women's World Cup was founded, and it has proven to be very popular. The U.S. has done very well, having won two of the first three tournaments. But on the men's side, it is not the same story, as the world's most powerful nation has never come close to winning. Instead, it is Brazil that has been dominant, having won the World Cup five times—while no other team has won more than three.

Men's World Cup, 1930–2002

Year	Winner	Final opponent	Site(s)	Year	Winner	Final opponent	Site(s)
1930	Uruguay	Argentina	Uruguay	1974	W. Germany	Netherlands	W. Germany
1934	Italy	Czechoslovakia	Italy	1978	Argentina	Netherlands	Argentina
1938	Italy	Hungary	France	1982	Italy	W. Germany	Spain
1950	Uruguay	Brazil	Brazil	1986	Argentina	W. Germany	Mexico
1954	W. Germany	Hungary	Switzerland	1990	W. Germany	Argentina	Italy
1958	Brazil	Sweden	Sweden	1994	Brazil	Italy	U.S.
1962	Brazil	Czechoslovakia	Chile	1998	France	Brazil	France
1966	England	W. Germany	England	2002	Brazil	Germany	Japan/ S. Korea
1970	Brazil	Italy	Mexico				

Questions to Ponder

1. Where and when is the World Cup tournament held?

2. What is the name of the group that founded the World Cup, and what made up this group?

3. Which countries have won consecutive World Cups?

4. What percent of the time has the nation hosting the World Cup won it? (Round to the nearest whole percent.)

5. Why do you think the World Cup is the world's biggest sporting event?

Better, Longer

When Jerry Rice was a rookie with the San Francisco 49ers in 1985, he wasn't sure if he could make it in the NFL. He dropped a lot of passes, and many of his team's own fans would boo him. But his team believed in him, and he kept working to be better. His work paid off, and in his second season Jerry led the NFL in receiving yards and touchdowns, and he was named the NFL's Offensive Player of the Year. From that point on, everyone agreed that he was the best receiver in football. In 1987 he eclipsed the single-season record of 18 receiving touchdowns by catching 22—and in only 12 games! At the end of the next season Jerry played in his first Super Bowl, where he set the record for receiving yards and was named the game's MVP as he led his team to victory.

Jerry helped the 49ers win two more Super Bowl in the 1990s (along the way setting almost every receiving record there is), but in the first game of the 1997 season he suffered the first and only major injury of his career and was basically lost for the season. Many players cannot come back from the injury Jerry suffered, but, as always, he worked hard, determined to be as good as he ever was. He succeeded, and the next season he was elected to the Pro Bowl (as he had been every year from 1986–1996). But the 49ers thought he was nearing the end of his career, and over the next two seasons they began to throw to him less. After 2000, Jerry signed with the Oakland Raiders, and in 2001 he had another 1,000-yard season, his 13th. In 2002, Jerry turned 40, which made him the only person that old to ever play his position. But age didn't seem to slow him down much, as he had yet *another* 1,000-yard season and was again elected to the Pro Bowl. No one knows how long Jerry Rice can continue to play football at such a high level, but he has been so good for so long that it seems impossible that anyone will ever exceed his lifetime totals.

Leading Lifetime Receivers (ranked by # of receptions; through 2002 season)

Player	Years	Receptions	Yards	Average	TDs
Jerry Rice	18	1,456	21,597	14.8	192
Cris Carter	16	1,101	13,899	12.6	130
Tim Brown	15	1,018	14,167	13.9	97
Andre Reed	16	951	13,198	13.9	87
Art Monk	16	940	12,721	13.5	68
Irving Fryar	17	851	12,785	15.0	84
Steve Largent	14	819	13,089	16.0	100
Henry Ellard	16	814	13,777	16.9	65
Larry Centers	13	808	6,691	8.3	27
James Lofton	16	764	14,004	18.3	75

Questions to Ponder

1. Who has the second-most receiving yards in history? How many less does he have than Rice?

2. Which player on the list has the highest yards-per-catch average?

3. What would be an average statistical season for Jerry Rice?

4. At the end of the 2002 season, what percentage of Jerry's total number of receptions did Cris Carter have? What percentage of his touchdowns?

5. Rice set out to be the best ever at his profession—and he succeeded; but in many professions there is not a such thing as being "the best," even if you are very good at what you do. What is a job you'd like to have? Is it something at which you (or anyone) can be "the best"? Why or why not?

Everyday Life

What's Inside . . . .

Taking Part

In democratic countries, the people decide who leads them. They do this by voting in elections. Elections are held at different times for different reasons, but usually there are at least one or two a year. This may not sound like something that's part of your everyday life, but what could be *more* a part of everyday life than the laws that govern us and the people who decide how a country runs?

Even though you get a chance to vote (or will when you're older, anyway) only a few times a year, voting responsibly takes a lot more time. This is because you need to know who and what you're voting for. There are many ways to do this. For example, if a president comes up for reelection, you would want to know what he or she has done while in office—and also something about the person or people running against him or her. You can do this by following the news and researching things about them online. You also get to vote for whether *propositions* (ideas for laws) will become laws, and also for how government money will be spent—and of course you would want to know about these, too, before casting your vote!

Surprisingly, many people don't look at voting as part of their everyday life, and instead they simply go to their polling place (where people vote) and vote—without really knowing what they're voting for. Even worse, many people don't vote at all! In Europe this is not so common, as more than 80% of people old enough to vote do so. In the United States, however, it is not the same, as even in presidential elections (when the largest number of people vote) only about 50% of the people take part. Many people do not even bother to register to vote (something you must do if you wish to vote), even though you can do this in many places, such as post offices and public libraries.

Voter Turnout in Presidential Elections, 1932–2000

Source: Federal Election Commission; Commission for Study of American Electorate; *Congressional Quarterly*

Year	Candidates	Voter Participation (% of voting-age population)	Year	Candidates	Voter Participation (% of voting-age population)
1932	Roosevelt-Hoover	52.4	1968	Nixon-Humphrey	60.9
1936	Roosevelt-Landon	56.0	1972	Nixon-McGovern	55.2[1]
1940	Roosevelt-Willkie	58.9	1976	Carter-Ford	53.5
1944	Roosevelt-Dewey	56.0	1980	Reagan-Carter	54.0
1948	Truman-Dewey	51.1	1984	Reagan-Mondale	53.1
1952	Eisenhower-Stevenson	61.6	1988	Bush-Dukakis	50.2
1956	Eisenhower-Stevenson	59.3	1992	Clinton-Bush-Perot	55.9
1960	Kennedy-Nixon	62.8	1996	Clinton-Dole-Perot	49.0
1964	Johnson-Goldwater	61.9	2000	Bush-Gore	51.3

(1) The sharp drop in 1972 followed the expansion of eligibility with the enfranchisement of 18- to 20-year-olds.

Questions to Ponder

1. Where do people go to vote?

2. Why can't you vote in elections right now?

3. What does it mean to do something "responsibly"?

4. In which U.S. presidential election since 1932 did the lowest percentage of eligible voters take part?

5. Some people say that in a country of millions one person's vote doesn't matter. Do you think this is true?

Knowing What You're Eating

Listing the ingredients of food products has been a regular practice for a very long time. But prior to 1990 U.S. law did not require the nutritional information about foods to be listed. Some companies did it on their own with some foods, but if you wanted to know how many calories or how much fat was in many foods, you wouldn't find that on the packaging. This changed with the Nutrition Labeling and Education Act. This requires food manufacturers to disclose the fat (saturated and unsaturated), cholesterol, sodium, sugar, fiber, protein, and carbohydrate content in their products.

Listing the ingredients of food products has long been considered very important, mainly because it is a way for people who are allergic to certain things to know whether those things are in what they're buying. For some people, that information can mean life or death! Nutritional information is not quite like that. However, in recent years society has become more aware of the importance of healthful eating—which includes things like not taking in too many calories, too much fat (especially saturated fat), too much cholesterol, or too much sodium. Today we understand better than ever what healthful eating is—and what years of poor eating habits can do to the body! This is why it became law that food products be labeled: so people would have a chance to keep track of what they eat. On the labels, you will find not only how much fat, cholesterol, etc., may be in a single serving (portion) of the food, but also what percentage that serving gives you of the total amount of these things that you should have every day. Part of the Nutrition Labeling and Education Act is that the food labeling be *standardized*, which means that it is always listed in the same way. This helps people to know exactly what to look for and how to read it. Whether they pay attention to it is up to them!

Sample Food Label

Nutrition Facts
Serving Size 1/2 cup (1 oz.) = (30g)
Servings per container 14

Amount Per Serving	Cereal	Cereal w/ 1/2 cup Lowfat Milk
Calories	**100**	**150**
Calories from Fat	**10**	**25**

	% Daily Value**	
Total Fat 1g*	2%	4%
Saturated Fat 0g	0%	5%
Cholesterol 0mg	0%	3%
Sodium 50mg	2%	5%
Total Carbohydrates 20g	7%	9%
Dietary Fiber 2g	8%	8%
Sugars 5g		
Protein 4g		

Vitamin A	0%	6%
Vitamin C	0%	2%
Calcium	0%	15%
Iron	2%	4%

* Amount in Cereal. One half cup lowfat milk contributes an additional 50 calories, 1.5g total fat (1g saturated fat), 9 mg cholesterol, 60mg sodium, 6g total carbohydrates (6g sugars), and 3g protein.
** Percents (%) of a Daily Value are based on a 2,000 calorie diet. Your Daily Values may vary higher or lower depending on your calorie needs:

Nutrient	Calories	2,000	2,500
Total Fat	Less than	65g	80g
Sat Fat	Less than	20g	25g
Cholesterol	Less than	300mg	300mg
Sodium	Less than	2,400mg	2,400mg
Total Carbohydrates		300g	375g
Dietary Fiber		25g	30g

Calories per gram:
Fat 9 • Carbohydrate 4 • Protein 4

Questions to Ponder

1. What is the name of the law that requires the labeling of the nutritional information of food products?

2. Name five pieces of nutritional information that you will always find in food labels.

3. If something is "required," what does that mean?

4. Look at the sample food label, which is for a type of cereal. If you ate the whole box of cereal (without milk) in one day, what percentage of the maximum amount of sodium you should have in one day would you have eaten?

5. It costs companies money to put the nutritional information on their packages—which makes the prices higher for us. Do you think paying more money for food is worth having the nutritional information? Why or why not?

Energy to Burn

We've all heard of calories, and we all know they have to do with food. But this is a little misleading. For starters, what we call a calorie when referring to food is actually a kilocalorie (kilo- = 1,000), or a "big calorie." And calories are actually a measure of energy—specifically (in the case of the kilocalorie), how much energy it takes to raise the temperature of 1 kilogram of water 1 degree C (Celsius).

Okay, so now we can define a calorie. But what does the energy have to do with food? Actually, another thing pretty much all of us know is that food is energy for the body—and now we're getting closer to understanding what calories really are! Think of calories as the energy value of food (which exists in three different forms: protein, fats, and carbohydrates). Here's how it works in practice: First, we eat. The energy in the food is released as the body breaks it down during digestion. Different parts of the food are used by the body in different ways. Protein, for example, is used to help build and repair body tissues (such as muscles). Calories don't tell us about how the body will use a particular food, just how much total energy is available for use.

If calories are just energy and we use energy every moment of our lives (even while we sleep!), how can someone take in too many? After all, would we ever say that we can have too much electricity? But the answer is "yes." Think about a lamp that takes a 100-watt bulb. If something goes wrong with the lamp and it draws too much energy from the outlet, too much will go into the bulb—which can burst! While nothing exactly like this happens with the body, if we take into our bodies more energy than the body can store for use, it builds up in bad ways. The most common of these is fat. While the body needs some fat—both in its diet and as part of the body itself—too much fat that the body can't use will produce more fat on the body than it needs. How many calories we need depends on our individual bodies and the way we use them. For example, someone who engages in long-distance running needs not only many more calories than most of us, but also more of a specific type—namely, those provided by carbohydrates, which provide the kind of energy needed for slow, prolonged activities. This is why marathoners "carbo-load" in the days before a race by eating foods especially high in carbohydrates, such as pasta. But there's more to it than even this, as the body can use certain types of carbohydrates and fats more efficiently than others—and so, just as with calories in general, the amount is only part of the story.

Energy to Burn *(cont.)*

Selected Foods and Caloric Value

Food (portion)	Wt. (g)	Protein (g)	Fat (g)	Carbohydrate (g)	Total Calories
Apple pie (1 slice)	158	3	18	60	405
Bagel, plain (1)	68	7	2	38	200
Banana (1)	114	1	1	27	105
Black beans (1 cup)	171	15	1	41	225
Bread, whole-wheat (1 slice)	28	3	1	13	70
Carrot (1)	72	1	0	7	30
Celery (1 stalk)	40	0	0	1	5
Cheese, cheddar (1 oz.)	28	7	9	0	115
Chicken, roasted/skinless (3 oz.)	86	27	3	0	140
Corn flakes (1 oz.)	28	2	0	24	110
Dill pickle (1)	65	0	0	1	5
Doughnut (1)	50	3	12	24	210
Egg, hard-boiled (1)	50	6	5	1	75
Ground beef, broiled (3 oz.)	85	20	18	0	245
Ham (3 oz.)	85	18	14	0	205
Ice cream (1 cup)	133	5	14	32	270
Milk chocolate (1 oz.)	28	2	9	16	145
Milk, skim (1 cup)	245	8	0	12	85
Milk, whole (1 cup)	244	8	8	11	150
Muffin, bran (1)	45	3	4	24	140
Orange juice (1 cup)	249	2	0	27	110
Peanuts (1 cup)	145	39	71	27	840
Pizza, cheese (1 slice)	120	15	9	39	290
Potato, baked (1)	156	3	0	34	145
Potato chips (10)	20	1	7	10	105
Rice, white (1 oz.)	28	2	0	25	110
Soda (12 fl. oz.)	369	0	0	41	160
Soup, chicken noodle (1 cup)	241	4	2	9	75
Spaghetti (2 oz.)	57	7	1	41	200
Spinach (1 cup)	180	5	0	7	40
Sugar, white (1 tsp.)	12	0	0	12	45
Water (12 fl. oz.)	370	0	0	0	0

Questions to Ponder

1. If you want to build muscles, which form of calories will help you do this best?

2. Which three of the foods listed above have the least caloric value?

3. How many grams are in 100 kilograms?

4. What would seem to account for the caloric difference between skim milk and whole milk?

5. Relative to their size and level of activity, babies need a very high caloric intake. Why do you think this is?

What You Get Paid
(At Least)

Today in many places there exists what is called a minimum wage. A minimum wage is the lowest amount of money per hour of work that a company is allowed to pay someone. They can pay them *more*, of course, just not less. The idea behind minimum wage is that there is a minimum amount of money that any person—no matter what his or her job—deserves to be paid for the time spent at work.

The first minimum wage was established in New Zealand in 1894. Australia followed a few years later, as did Great Britain about a decade later. The first minimum-wage law in the United States was a 1912 state law put into place in Massachusetts. Eight other states did the same thing a year later. However, a Supreme Court decision in 1923 threw out the state laws, and it was not until 1938 that the U.S. passed a federal law (one that applies to the country as a whole), setting the minimum wage at 25¢ per hour for most workers.

As the cost of living has gone up, so has the minimum wage. However, the minimum wage is not enough for most people to live on. Some people think this is okay, since they feel that jobs that pay only minimum wage are not the kinds of jobs people who need to support themselves should have. Others, though, feel that every job should pay enough for people to live on, and they want the government to pass a law that raises the minimum wage to that point, turning it into what they call "a livable wage."

Changes in U.S. Federal Minimum Wage Since 1950

Date of Change	Wage ($/hour)	Date of Change	Wage ($/hour)
1/25/50	.75	1/1/78	2.65
3/1/56	1.00	1/1/79	2.90
9/3/61	1.15	1/1/80	3.10
9/3/63	1.25	1/1/81	3.35
2/1/67	1.40	4/1/90	3.80
2/1/68	1.60	4/1/91	4.25
5/1/74	2.00	10/1/96	4.75
1/1/75	2.10	9/1/97	5.15
1/1/76	2.30		

Questions to Ponder

1. Where and when was the first minimum wage?

2. In 1938 how many hours would an American earning minimum wage have needed to work to make $100?

3. Why didn't the minimum-wage law put into place in Massachusetts in 1912 apply to the other 49 states?

4. Since 1950 in the U.S., when was there the greatest percentage increase in the minimum wage? What percent was the increase?

5. Do you think the minimum wage should be a livable wage? Give a reason for your position— then give a reason why someone might have an opposite opinion.

You Can't Hide from Taxes

Almost everyone hates taxes. Almost no matter where you live in the world, taxes are something you can't avoid. When you work, taxes are taken out of what you earn. When you buy something, the cost is often higher because of taxes. If you own a business, you pay taxes just for having a business. It's no wonder taxes are hated! But taxes are a lot more than the government simply taking your money just for fun.

First of all, what exactly are taxes? Basically, a tax is an amount of money you pay. Different kinds of taxes are paid in different ways. Income taxes, for example, are taken out of the check you get from your job. The government takes this money to pay for services it provides for the people, including things like paying for police and fire departments, building and fixing roads, and the military. This is how governments get most of the money they need to function. How much income tax you pay depends on how much money you make: the more you make, the more you pay. You also must pay income tax on interest, which is money banks give you for keeping your money in them. Another tax taken out of your paycheck is called Social Security. This money is used for pensions that workers can get when they retire or become disabled or that their families can get when the workers die.

A different kind of tax is called sales tax. Most of the things you buy in most places cost more than the prices listed because sales tax is added to them. A sales tax is based on a certain percentage of the price of whatever you're buying. For example, if a state has an 8% sales tax and the item you want to buy costs $20, the total amount you end up paying is $21.60. Luckily, food is the one thing that you usually don't pay sales tax on . . . except when you eat in a restaurant. Otherwise, it would be a lot more expensive to live!

Tax Burden in Selected Countries*

Country	% of Income**	Country	% of Income**	Country	% of Income**
Austria	28	Greece	18	Norway	29
Australia	23	Hungary	32	Poland	31
Belgium	42	Iceland	21	Portugal	18
Brazil	34	Ireland	20	Spain	18
Canada	27	Italy	29	Sweden	33
Czech Republic	23	Japan	16	Switzerland	21
Denmark	44	Korea	9	Turkey	29
Finland	34	Mexico	3	United Kingdom	24
France	27	Netherlands	36	United States	26
Germany	42	New Zealand	19		

*does not include sales tax
**based on an average income

Questions to Ponder

1. Name three things the government uses income taxes to pay for.
2. What is the name of the tax you pay when you buy something?
3. If you hate taxes, which of the above countries is the worst one for you to live in? Which is the best?
4. If you get injured on the job and are unable to work, the government will give you money to help you out. Where does it get the money it will give you?
5. Many people do not think taxes are a good thing, and there are some places in the world that do not have certain kinds of taxes. Do you think taxes are a necessary thing? Why or why not?

Talking While on the Move

It wasn't so long ago that you had two options if you needed to call someone: find a pay phone, or go home. Has your car broken down by the side of the road? Better start walking! But we have something today that has changed all of that, making our lives both safer and more convenient: the cellular radio telephone, or (as we call it today) cell phone. The cell phone was developed in the late 1970s. Even though the first ones were not very good, they were a great success. The reason is obvious: it's more convenient to make a phone call from wherever you are than to be forced to find a phone.

❖❖❖ It's a Fact! ❖❖❖

New York is the first state to ban using hand-held cell phones while driving. In 2003, New York City became the first U.S. city to pass a law fining patrons of theaters and concerts for the use cell phones during a performance.

By the mid 1990s cell phones were much better—and more and more people were using them. Cell phones help people to be safe, because having one means that you can call for help whenever and wherever you need it. Cell phones also make life more convenient. If you go to the supermarket and forget what your mother told you to buy, you can simply call her from the middle of the store. If you're driving to someone's house but can't find it, you can call and ask the person how to get there. Cell phones have even changed how people walk around, because you can be out for a walk in the California sun while talking to a friend who is looking at the New York skyline. And someone can call you on a cell phone, and reach you wherever you are. Cell phones make it easier for us to stay in touch with each other.

Nevertheless, all the news about cell phones is not positive. As cell phones have become more widely used in recent years, complaints about them have become more and more widespread—especially about their use in automobiles. Some recent studies seem to show that many serious accidents occur while drivers are talking on cell phones. The suggestion is that drivers are distracted by their conversations; the process of punching in a number; or by simply looking away from traffic to pick up the phone from a pocket, purse, or car seat. Less serious complaints come from patrons in restaurants and theaters who do not appreciate a nearby diner rudely carrying on a loud personal conversation at the next table or persons in theaters or concerts whose phones ring in the middle of performances. In fact, some cities have passed laws that fine people for the use of a cell phone under just such conditions as those mentioned above. It may be that the cell phone, like other technological achievements, is a double-edged sword. For all its many advantages, it seems that the cell phone is a mixed blessing—regarded by some as a great asset and by others as a public nuisance, or worse yet, as a threat to public safety.

Questions to Ponder

1. What is "cell phone" short for?
2. When were cell phones first developed?
3. What seems to be the most serious charge against cell phone use?
4. Name two other technological advancements that are "double-edged swords" and explain your choices, along with the meaning of that term.
5. What is the main reason you like having or would like to have a cell phone? Explain why this is important to you.

Understanding Blood Pressure

When you go to the doctor, what is one of the first things the nurse always does? He or she usually puts a little sleeve around your arm, and then what happens? The sleeve tightens. As it does this, the nurse puts a stethoscope on your arm—just below the tightening sleeve—and listens. The sleeve gets tighter and tighter, and then it releases. By now, you probably know that what the nurse is doing is taking your blood pressure. You also probably remember that the nurse tells you two numbers, and the first number is always larger than the second. But do you know what those numbers mean?

The blood pressure reading consists of two measurements (those two numbers the nurse tells you). The first number measures *systolic pressure*. This represents the amount of pressure in the blood vessels when the heart contracts and pushes blood through the circulatory system. In other words, it measures the maximum amount of pressure in one of your arteries while your heart is beating. The second number measures *diastolic pressure*, and it represents the pressure in the blood vessels in between beats. So, this second number is the maximum amount of pressure in one of your arteries while your heart is resting.

> ◇◇◇**It's a Fact!**◇◇◇
>
> For more than a century, blood pressure has been measured in terms of millimeters of mercury, which is a dangerous, highly toxic substance. Because of the rare, but not impossible, dangers associated with mercury spillage, many of the older monitors have been replaced by electronic devices. These newer measuring devices are much safer but not as reliable.

Taking one's blood pressure can be an important step in judging one's overall health. If a person's blood pressure is too high (see chart below) on a consistent basis, his or her doctor will prescribe diet, exercise, and medication to control the problem.

Systolic Pressure	Diastolic Pressure	What It Means
below 130	below 85	Normal
131–139	86–89	High Normal
140–159	90–99	High: Stage 1
160–179	100–109	High: Stage 2
above 180	above 110	High: Stage 3

Questions to Ponder

1. What are three ways to help control high blood pressure?
2. Diastolic pressure measures the amount of pressure in your arteries while your heart is _____.
   a. resting   b. beating   (*Fill in blank.*)
3. If a person's blood pressure is 128/88, what does it mean?
4. If measuring devices that use mercury are so reliable, why would anyone want to use less-reliable electronic devices?
5. What could be another title for this article?

Vacation 'Round the World

Right now you're in school. You probably go for about eight or nine months a year, then get the rest of the time off. When you go on vacation, it's probably with your parents. What you may realize but have never thought about is exactly how and when your parents get their time off so that they can go on vacation with you.

◇◇◇It's a Fact!◇◇◇

The days that the largest numbers of people get off are federal holidays, which are days that the government of a country recognizes. On those days— for example, New Year's Day (January 1) in the U.S. and many other countries—government offices are closed, as are most businesses. However, businesses are not required to be closed on these days. In fact, there are certain jobs which must have people working 24 hours a day, seven days a week. These are sometimes called *essential services* because society needs them. They include police and fire departments and hospitals.

When you have a job, you don't get as much time off as you do when you're in school. In fact, a full-time job (which usually means eight hours a day, five days a week) is something that people work at all year. But everyone needs some time off, whether it's from school or from work. In every country there are certain days that most people get off from work, but usually this amounts to only a few days per year. Employers (people or companies that hire people to work for them) know that this is not enough, and so they also give their employees (workers) vacation days. However, throughout the world different countries do not seem to agree about how much time off people should have. For example, if you live and work in Canada, you will probably get about four weeks of vacation time per year. However, just south of the border, you will get about half that much. In fact, the United States is known around the world as one of the countries that gives its workers the least amount of time off. Some people feel that workers in the U.S. would be better off if this country that leads the world in so many ways would follow the example of others when it comes to giving its workers time off!

Average Number of Vacation Days (by Country)					
Austria	30	Ireland	28	Portugal	25
Belgium	24	Italy	42	Spain	30
Brazil	34	Japan	25	Sweden	32
Canada	26	Korea	25	Switzerland	20
Denmark	30	Netherlands	25	United Kingdom	28
France	37	Norway	21	United States	14
Germany	35				

Questions to Ponder

1. How many hours per week do people generally work at full-time jobs?

2. Which country from those listed above is the best for getting time off? Which is the third-worst?

3. What does "essential" mean?

4. What is the average number of vacation days of all the countries listed above? (Round to the nearest whole number.)

5. How much vacation time do you think employees need? Do you think the kind of work they do makes a difference? Explain your answer.

Answer Key

Note: Answers will vary for #5 questions.

World History and Culture

Talk Is Old (p. 8)
1. a group of languages with common roots, (or) a group of languages which came from a common ancestor language
2. none
3. about 60
4. 1.022 billion

The First Bill of Rights (p. 9)
1. freedoms
2. eight
3. a system of words or language used for a particular subject; "term"
4. no; you can tell that England has existed since at least some years before 1215

Afghanistan: Surviving Oppression (p. 10)
1. 59 years (1919–1978)
2. fame, importance
3. a group (of people, countries, etc.) working together for a common cause
4. the Hindu Kush mountain range, the Khyber Pass

The Birth of the Presidency (p. 11)
1. because he knew that, as the first president, what he did while in office would be the model for the presidency in the future
2. because he believed in the Constitutional independence of the three branches of government
3. that they don't really want to do it, that they'd rather not
4. At the time, there was no limit.

The Law of the Land (p. 12)
1. the judicial
2. nine months
3. so that they are unable to be influenced by any outside forces when deciding cases
4. *Miranda v. Ohio; Gideon v. Wainwright*

The Great Soul (p. 13)
1. Great Britain
2. South Africa; to practice law
3. passive resistance, civil disobedience, non-cooperation, *Satyagraha* (at least one of these)
4. resisting or disobeying without fighting

The Nobel Prizes (p. 14)
1. someone who believes war is unjustified and that disputes should be settled only by peaceful means
2. $9.57 million
3. to leave (money, property, etc.) to another by means of a will; to hand down after death
4. Marie Curie, Albert Einstein

High and Low (p. 15)
1. China
2. a theocracy
3. 44 years
4. about 2.4 million

The Cold War (p. 16)
1. democracy and communism
2. containment
3. 69
4. Korea, Vietnam, Greece, Turkey, Afghanistan

Science and Technology

The Productive Revolution (p. 19)
1. at the beginning of the 18th century
2. the textile industry
3. the steam engine
4. It led to many people moving from the country to cities.

Bridging the Gap (p. 20)
1. suspension bridge
2. span
3. the 1990s; 50%
4. 20

Turning Water into Electricity (p. 21)
1. 1882; Appleton, WI
2. advancements in construction, machinery, and our understanding of electricity
3. Russia
4. 16%

How Film Came to Be (p. 22)
1. a mistaken perception of reality
2. chronophone, 1902
3. instrument for viewing
4. video, digital

The Most Famous Scientist (p. 23)
1. that I am very smart
2. 76
3. involving or causing great change; completely new
4. that matter and energy are really the same thing

The Computer Age (p. 24)
1. Charles Babbage
2. smaller, faster, cheaper
3. 186 years
4. 1 billion

Harnessing the Atom (p. 25)
1. a great deal of energy can be produced from a small amount of material
2. fission and fusion. Fission is the splitting of atomic nuclei, whereas fusion is the combining of nuclei.
3. problem, shortcoming
4. seven

Living Longer (p. 26)
1. 30 years
2. about 208% longer
$$[(77- 25) / 25 = 2.08]$$
3. knowledge and technology
4. remove, get rid of

The Net Around the World (p. 27)
1. ARPANET
2. Tim Berners-Lee
3. 20 years
4. 55 1/3 times more

Eye in the Sky (p. 28)
1. 377
2. Isaac Newton, 1668

Answer Key *(cont.)*

3. There was a problem with its mirror that kept the images from being as good as they should have been; $3 billion
4. clear, able to be seen through

The Natural World
The Building Blocks of Everything (p. 30)
1. oxygen atoms
2. the 19th/the 1800s
3. one carbon atom with two oxygen atoms
4. because there are patterns in the atomic make-up of the elements, and so they know—as Mendeleyev was the first to realize—that there must be elements to complete the patterns

Not *the* Solar System, Just Ours (p. 32)
1. having to do with a sun
2. 102 moons
3. H (i.e., hydrogen)
4. Venus and Earth

It's About Where on Earth You Are (p. 33)
1. it's location (where it is)
2. a beach on the equator
3. The climate of an area has a lot to do with where on Earth a place is in relation to where the sun is.
4. yes, because then the equator would be a vertical zone running around the middle of the planet—and the north pole would be right on it

Waves of Energy (p. 34)
1. radio waves; gamma rays
2. no: visible light
3. The wavelength of infrared is beneath that of red visible light, and the wavelength of ultraviolet is beyond that of violet visible light. (Accept any phrasing that demonstrates an understanding of the basic idea.)
4. UV rays are ultraviolet radiation. UV rays have a

wavelength longer X-Rays but shorter than visible light. (Accept any phrasing that demonstrates an understanding of the basic idea.)

Space Is Curved (p. 35)
1. gravity
2. that it is the curving of space caused by the mass of an object
3. a major advance or discovery
4. The farther you got away from Earth, the less gravity you would feel. This is because the space would be less and less curved by the Earth's mass as you got farther away.

Fire: What Is It? (p. 36)
1. by friction, by percussion, and by using a lens
2. anything that will burn (combustible material)
3. flint
4. that they were made to move so fast that they started breaking apart from each other

The Northern (and Southern) Lights (p. 37)
1. within 30 degrees latitude of each of the poles
2. the polar lights; a comet's tail
3. lights
4. It collides with gas particles in Earth's atmosphere, which excites them, causing them to give off light.

The Cheetah and the Snail (p. 38)
1. rabbits
2. 2.5 times
3. black mamba snake
4. b. 2,500 years

World Geography and Travel
Be a World Traveler (p.40)
1. 6,250 miles
2. 1 mile
3. 1,998 miles
4. Cairo

From Country to Country (p. 41)
1. A passport is a request from one government to allow the holder of the passport to travel safely

through another country.
2. whenever you want to enter a foreign country that does not have a special agreement with your government allowing you to enter without a passport
3. permission from a foreign country to enter it (in the form of a stamp)
4. about 2,450 years

Why They're There (p. 42)
1. crustal uplift and volcanism
2. 19,195 feet
3. of or pertaining to the Earth
4. that they are part of the same mountain range

Country or Continent? (p. 43)
1. Jan. 1, 1901
2. Antarctica
3. 1,150
4. the Netherlands

World's Tallest Buildings (p. 44)
1. Sears Tower; Chicago, IL, U.S.
2. Commerzbank Tower; 981 feet; Frankfurt, Germany
3. Empire State Building; 1931; New York, NY, U.S.
4. 16.85 feet

Water Falls (p. 45)
1. erosion of the weaker part of a streambed
2. a cascade
3. two
4. You can't tell anything about its volume, except that it has some. This is because neither height nor location tell you anything about volume. The reason you know it has some volume is that, for it to be a waterfall, some amount of water must be flowing over the falls.

The Undersea Train (p. 46)
1. It runs between England and France underneath the English Channel.
2. 192 years
3. Eurotunnel
4. about 18 minutes

Answer Key (cont.)

THE WORLD ALMANAC

Frontier Forests (p. 47)

1. forest ecosystems that are still in their original condition
2. almost half; about 20%
3. by each country's percentage of the world's total frontier forest area
4. Canada and Venezuela

The Bottom of the World (p. 48)

1. none
2. opposite of
3. 90%
4. airplanes

From Fiction to Fact (p. 50)

1. Jules Verne
2. 17 years
3. *The New York World*
4. 1,280

The Arts

Award-Winning Books (p. 52)

1. Lois Lowry
2. *Juvenile* means intended for children or young people.
3. an 18th-century bookseller who wrote and published children's books
4. Answers will vary.

The King of Museums (p. 53)

1. Paris, France (on the right bank of the Seine River)
2. 111 years
3. Leonardo da Vinci
4. to contain, to have inside, to hold

The Boss (p. 54)

1. yes; John Ford and Joseph L. Mankiewicz
2. Frank Borzage; 1932
3. 1940s and 1950s; eight
4. consisting of, made up of, containing

Not Exactly a Failure (p. 55)

1. the Netherlands
2. from his brother Theo
3. 97 years
4. 1/825,000

More Than a Pop Group (p. 56)

1. England
2. Paul McCartney and John Lennon

3. 50%
4. first group of the "British Invasion," first album recorded in stereo, first worldwide TV program, first group to have #s 1–5 on pop singles charts (any two)

Challenging Freedom (p. 57)

1. It is not allowed wherever it is banned; it is forbidden.
2. the First Amendment of the Bill of Rights
3. good, works well
4. Judy Blume, Lois Lowry

Not Just a Wide Street (p. 58)

1. New York City
2. puts on plays and musicals
3. Tony Kushner and Terrence McNally
4. *Travesties*

Better Ways to Listen (p. 59)

1. records
2. They don't wear out, the sound quality is better, you can easily skip from song to song (any two).
3. cassette singles
4. Their sales went up while sales of all others went down.

Keeping Parents Informed (p. 60)

1. V
2. 31 years
3. two: TV-14 and TV-MA
4. twice: in the upper left corner of the screen for the first 15 seconds of the first and second hours

Numbers and Statistics

The Perpetual Calendar (p. 62)

1. seven
2. a general law or rule
3. Friday
4. There is none, because Leap Day is February 29, and so a leap year is the same as a regular year until after February 28.

Who Is Dow Jones? (p. 64)

1. Charles Dow and Henry Jones, two financial reporters

2. 30
3. the New York Stock Exchange
4. $1,013.84

Keeping Track (p. 66)

1. 1665
2. once every 10 years
3. no; There are records of censuses dating back to 3800 B.C.
4. about .33%

Exchanging Money for Money (p. 67)

1. foreign exchange
2. because Japan doesn't use U.S. dollars; instead, they use yen
3. You will have to spend more dollars this year than last to get the same amount of rubles.
4. 693.77; 87.28

The Electoral College (p. 68)

1. the first Monday after the second Wednesday in the December after a presidential election
2. California; 55
3. three
4. none

The Cost of Living, Then and Now (p. 69)

1. because things are more expensive now
2. someone who buys and uses things
3. No, because these are not necessary for day-to-day living.
4. 932%

Who's Watching What (p. 70)

1. it surveys a representative sampling of the population
2. to find out, to establish precisely
3. the Super Bowl
4. because in 1994 there were more TVs than in 1980, and so even though more TVs were tuned into the '94 show, the '80 show had a higher percentage of the total number of TVs tuned into it

**The Zoning Improvement
Program (p. 71)**
1. 1963
2. three
3. a word made out of the first
   letters of other words
4. 4; 4

Sports

Trophies of the NHL (p. 73)
1. Montreal Canadians
2. b. Frank Nighbor
3. Washington, D.C.
4. Answers will vary.

The World Plays Here (p. 74)
1. 25%
2. Nikoloz Tskitishvili, Bostjan
   Nachbar; Italy
3. 3
4. Hakeem Olajuwon; Nigeria

The Greatest (p. 75)
1. Cassius Clay
2. Islam; shortly after winning the
   heavyweight championship in
   1964
3. their moral beliefs
4. He threw his gold medal in a
   river, and he refused to take part
   in the draft for the Vietnam War.

***The* Bicycle Race (p. 76)**
1. Paris
2. Jacques Anquetil, Eddy Merckx,
   and Lance Armstrong; four
3. the Olympics
4. France; 42%

The Triple Crown (p. 77)
1. Thoroughbreds
2. England (Great Britain)
3. 3 15/16 miles
4. three, because only three-year-
   olds are allowed to compete in
   Triple Crown races

It's All About Speed (p. 78)
1. any competition involving cars
2. Breedlove
3. a rocket-powered one
4. 11.6 times faster

Comparing Pitchers (p. 79)
1. because it takes into account
   only how effective they are
   against batters and not how good
   their team is
2. a general period of time
3. 1900–'19
4. 2.76

**The World's Fastest Human
(p. 80)**
1. whoever runs the 100 meters the
   fastest at the Olympics
2. because it is long enough to
   allow athletes to reach their
   maximum speed but short
   enough so that they can
   maintain that speed throughout
   the race
3. Donovan Bailey, 9.84 seconds
4. 63%

**The Biggest Sporting Event
(p. 81)**
1. a different place, every four
   years
2. FIFA, seven European countries
3. Italy and Brazil
4. 35%

Better, Longer (p. 82)
1. Tim Brown; 7,430
2. James Lofton
3. 81 rec., 1,200 yds., 11 TDs
4. 75.6%; 67.7%

Everyday Living

Taking Part (p. 84)
1. polling places
2. because I'm not old enough
3. to do it in the right or correct
   way; knowing what you're
   doing
4. 1996

**Knowing What You're Eating
(p. 85)**
1. Nutrition Labeling and
   Education Act
2. fat (both saturated and
   unsaturated), cholesterol,
   sodium, sugar, fiber, protein,
   carbohydrate (any five)

3. It is necessary, it has to be done
   (etc.).
4. 28%

Energy to Burn (p. 86)
1. protein
2. water, celery, dill pickle
3. 100,000
4. Whole milk has fat calories,
   while skim milk does not.

**What You Get Paid (At Least)
(p. 88)**
1. New Zealand, 1894
2. 400 hours
3. because it was a state law and
   not a federal one
4. 3/1/56; 33%

**You Can't Hide from Taxes
(p. 89)**
1. police dept., fire dept., road
   maintenance, military (any
   three)
2. sales tax
3. Denmark; Mexico
4. Social Security taxes

**Talking While on the Move
(p. 90)**
1. cellular radio telephone
2. the late 1970s
3. They can cause car accidents.
4. A "double-edged sword" can
   benefit you but also harm you.

**Understanding Blood Pressure
(p. 91)**
1. diet, exercise, and medication
2. a. resting
3. His or her systolic pressure is
   normal, but the diastolic
   pressure is high normal.
4. Mercury is highly toxic.

**Vacation 'Round the World
(p. 92)**
1. 40
2. Italy; Norway
3. necessary, needed
4. 28